Helen Armitage is a writer and book editor with an MA in Screenwriting and Screen Research. She has a lifelong interest in natural history and is drawn to rural wild places. She edited the Royal Horticultural Society's *A Passion for Plants* that accompanied the BBC TV series and worked at Kew's Herbarium on Earthscan's *The Commercial Uses of Biodiversity*. She lives in an area of London that was once part of the Great North Wood. Along the highest section of the London clay ridge that runs through it, two ospreys are on record as having been seen during spring migration.

LADY
OF THE LOCH

HELEN ARMITAGE

Constable • London

Constable & Robinson Ltd
3 The Lanchesters
162 Fulham Palace Road
London W6 9ER
www.constablerobinson.com

First published in the UK by Constable,
an imprint of Constable & Robinson Ltd, 2011

A copy of the British Library Cataloguing in
Publication data is available from the British Library

ISBN 978-1-84901-702-2

Typeset by TW Typesetting, Plymouth, Devon

Printed and bound in the EU

1 3 5 7 9 10 8 6 4 2

For Gary

Contents

Foreword

I first came into contact with ospreys in the 1970s when I was a teenager undertaking some voluntary work with the Scottish Wildlife Trust at Loch of the Lowes. Now, as the Scottish Wildlife Trust's chief executive, I am delighted to have been asked to write a foreword to this inspiring account of the bird believed to be Scotland's oldest osprey, a summer resident at Loch of the Lowes.

The return of the osprey to Scotland is a major conservation success story and represents a beacon of hope as we strive to rebuild our beleaguered biodiversity and battered ecosystems. Helen Armitage reveals the astonishing life of one of our most impressive and high-profile birds in a tale that involves surviving twenty round trips of 6,000 miles to West Africa and raising forty-eight chicks. It is the story of a bird that became a member of a Perthshire community and whose successes and tribulations have been followed by people all over the world.

The book is also a tribute to all those who have played, and continue to play, a part in ensuring the survival of Scottish ospreys, particularly those who have spent so many nights on osprey-watch, guarding nests against egg thieves and other vandals. The conspicuous devotion of these frontline, unpaid enthusiasts to the conservation of Scotland's wildlife and wild places has had a significant influence on my own development, and instilled in me a huge respect for conservation volunteers.

The return of the osprey, and attendant viewing and interpretation opportunities created by the Scottish Wildlife Trust and the RSPB, has delighted and inspired generations of people and helped to build much needed support for Scotland's conservation programmes. Helen has produced a valuable insight into the history of the osprey in Scotland and I am very confident that this intimate and absorbing account of the bird that became known as 'Lady' will inspire even more people to delight in the intrinsic value of our native wildlife and to support nature conservation.

Simon Milne MBE, chief executive,
Scottish Wildlife Trust
Edinburgh 2011

1 The magic of ospreys

To everything there is a season, and a time and purpose. For Lady, Britain's oldest breeding osprey, summer's end was her time to leave her Scottish nesting grounds. It marked the close of the ospreys' annual breeding season and the start of their long flight south to autumn and winter in West Africa. That year, 2009, proved no exception to a routine that Lady had established over almost two decades: she would depart the Scottish Wildlife Trust's Loch of the Lowes nature reserve in late July or early August to undertake her three-thousand-mile autumn migration.

By the middle of August, Lady was no longer to be seen on her scenic nest overlooking tree-lined, reed-fringed Loch of the Lowes, attending to her almost fully grown chicks, or in flight above its fish-laden waters, or perched in one of her favourite trees in the surrounding woodland. Soon confirmation came from the Lowes reserve, where Lady had arrived in March, that their female osprey had indeed departed that year for tropical Senegal or Gambia. This was Africa at an ecological crossroads, the countries straddling a transition zone that supported a mosaic of habitats suited to a diverse range of birds, with the ospreys – and Lady – among them.

As she had done each year for almost twenty years, Lady had spent the spring and summer of 2009 on her nest at Lowes. From the reserve's visitor centre it was easy to see the shambolic-looking latticework of fat sticks, as capacious as a double bed, set sixty-foot high atop a blue-green Scots pine. From that familiar nest, in which she had raised a record number of chicks, she had stretched her wings one last time in August. Lifting herself skyward, she had likely moved off with powerful wingbeats to fly high above the woods that encircled the loch. For anyone watching from the Lowes observation hides or out walking or working in the surrounding woods, fields or hillsides in that corner of Perthshire, she would have been hard to miss: a big bird, flashing by in a gleam of white and chocolate brown, with a distinctive five-foot wingspan. Sharp eyes or strong binoculars might have spotted her identifying 'highwayman's mask', the band or stripe of dark brown feathers that extended around her bright lemon yellow eyes to the back of her head, or the characteristic female breastband of her upper chest, a wide necklace of heavily speckled feathers that lay just above her white chest.

But now that she had gone, what the eye could not see

the heart still grieved for: Lady's absence hung heavy, as it did every year at Lowes after she abandoned Scottish skies for Africa. She had earned a reputation over the years as a characterful bird and had captured the public imagination. For years, she and her ever-increasing osprey family had excited interest, curiosity and passion, locally, nationally and, indeed, internationally. In Lowes' nearest town of Dunkeld, the ninth-century capital of the new nation created by the union of the Scots and Picts, everyone followed her progress with interest, discussing her regularly in the streets and cafés. Locals had known of Lady for years; some had even participated in the annual osprey watch to protect her eggs from collectors each breeding season, day and night.

They looked forward to her presence in Lowes' skies each spring and summer, swooping, soaring high on fixed wing over the ever-changing waters of the loch, and delighted in watching her flight, direct and purposeful, high above the reserve's dense, encircling woodland where she had nested since 1991. Lady was a practised parent: she had spent many a long day building, breeding, defending, feeding, as if her work were never done. Then perching motionless, yet eternally watchful, on a lofty lookout post.

Whether circling, flapping, hovering or still, Lady had an enviable bird's eye view of the Perthshire landscape. The county over which she flew sits at the heart of mainland Scotland and includes the heather-clad peaks of the Trossachs – the Highlands in miniature. It is an ancient land, comprising the early Celtic earldoms of Atholl, Breadalbane, Gowrie, Strathearn, Mentieth and Balquhidder. Lowes itself lies in the earldom of Atholl, once the area of Clan Duncan, who supported Duncan I, murdered by Macbeth. When the line became extinct in the early thirteenth century, the region and the earldom reverted to the Crown until the mid-1400s, when James II of Scotland bestowed the title on a Stewart of Balvenie. Later Queen Anne raised it to a dukedom. The seat of the earls and dukes of Atholl is the turreted Blair Castle, which dates from the thirteenth century, and is close to the Grampian Mountains, a strategic location on the route north to Inverness. It was once a threatening, dangerous place, but is now a landscape of wild, natural beauty.

Dunkeld is typical of Perthshire's numerous age-old settlements. An attractive town, with a long and dramatic history, it was made the seat of the Scottish primacy in AD 851 by Kenneth MacAlpin, first king of Scots, and was once the ecclesiastical centre of Scotland. A battle raged around Dunkeld Cathedral during the Jacobite uprising of 1689 but now it is a peaceful place, with lawns that slope down to the river. The town lies several miles north of Perth in the hilly, rugged countryside of the southern Grampians, nestled in a valley, enclosed by woody crags and watered by the Tay. The magnificent lochs, mountains and glens make it a haven for ospreys.

The Scottish Wildlife Trust bought the 250-acre site at Lowes in April 1969, mostly for its aquatic habitat: Loch of

4

the Lowes is a mesotrophic loch that supports a rich flora, including slender naiad, *Najas flexillis*, an internationally protected species. There are various habitats in the Lunan Lochs water basin, of which Loch of the Lowes is part, including a watershed and surrounding mountainous upland, with heath and heather at the top. The watershed is quite large, and feeds into the glacial valley. There are wetlands and reed beds, and water lilies feature widely – yellow and white – among all manner of plant life.

The reserve is set in a good mix of woodland, with native species of fir, Scots pine in particular, plus non-native trees – there is lots of hazel, willow and birch, which are regenerative, and some beech, which some say is native now because it has been there so long. All these different elements contribute to the health and welfare of the entire region, which is important in the wider ecology.

The osprey became a vital part of that eclectic mix following their arrival at Lowes that April too. It is impossible to support a top-order predator like the osprey without healthy populations beneath it – of fish, pond life, insects – that rely on algae balance and nutrient run-off, which in turn require the cooperation of the surrounding farms and landowners. It is a bigger-picture scenario: the osprey's existence relies on a great deal of furious paddling beneath the surface to support the birds. That the osprey are doing so well in Scotland, and anywhere else that they are now thriving, is testament to a carefully managed environment.

* * *

From time to time during the late summer of 2009, after Lady's departure, another female osprey was spotted at Lowes. Could it be Lady? No: Lady had headed south on a migration that would take her more than a month to complete, one of a series she had made from Lowes to her overwintering grounds in equatorial West Africa. Indeed, most ospreys that nest across the Palaearctic (the biogeographical region that includes the cold and temperate zones of the Old World – Europe, North Africa and Asia north of the Himalayas) winter south of twenty degrees north, in Africa, India and South East Asia. Ospreys from elsewhere, subspecies from North America, the Caribbean and Australasia, do things differently – although, remarkably, they remain one species and look similar to their northerly relatives. The osprey ranges widely over four continents but it has, unusually, withstood speciation, or the formation of new and distinct species, in the course of evolution over more than fifteen million years.

Palaearctic ospreys, like Lady, that nest in Scotland, as well as those that breed in northern Scandinavia, Germany, Russia, Poland, Asia east to Kamchatka and Japan, travel long distances on their spring and autumn migrations. Those found nesting in North America overwinter in Central and South America. But ospreys are known to be partial migrants, in that not all of them migrate so far. Those found in coastal Australia, for instance, move only short distances after breeding, relocating to non-breeding quarters a few hundred miles or so inland. Ospreys in residence along the shores of the Mediterranean, the Red Sea and the Persian Gulf are also generally non-migratory.

On her journey south from Lowes, Lady had many natural geographic obstacles to overcome, including some vast stretches of ocean and desert. When it comes to ease of migration, flying over water is not ideal: it does not create the best conditions for soaring flight on fixed wing, as opposed to the more tiring wing flapping. It lacks the updraughts and rising currents of relatively warm air, or thermals, that birds need to gain height. Some birds prefer not to cross stretches of water for this reason, but ospreys are not among them. They are also quite prepared to traverse the driest desert to reach their wintering grounds, which, for ospreys like Lady, meant the demanding 1,250-mile journey across the Sahara. This vast, arid section of Lady's marathon migration was an ordeal in itself, made in a single flight lasting from thirty-six hours to two and a half days at twenty to thirty miles per hour. Ospreys can and do fly actively, not just soaring – their narrow, high-loading wing design facilitates this – and are known to do so without the advantage of thermals, which are absent, for instance, at dusk and dawn. During any lengthy water or desert crossing, ospreys fly by night, but they do most of their migration during the day.

In 2009 the journey Lady faced was one she had done numerous times on her own, as ospreys do, and Lowes looked forward to seeing her again the following March: while the timing of her departure was consistent, so was her return. However, her advanced age – approaching her mid-twenties – made this ever less likely, so as each year passed her presence was ever more treasured.

Lowes had some adjusting to do in late August without its star osprey, especially once Lady's mate and their chicks had left too. The osprey has a certain mystique: it is handsome and spectacular to watch, a returned wanderer, a bird once driven out and now restored to its native lands, back from the brink of extinction to breed again on British shores after a long absence. With its relative rarity, its large size, its fabulous flight and fishing skills, it is a hard act to follow, but each species of bird makes its own unique contribution and, that autumn, others remained or arrived at Lowes to engage and fascinate.

By mid-November flocks of fieldfare and redwing, both winter visitors, were mingling on the rowan trees at the front of Lowes' visitor centre. At the reserve's peanut feeders two jays, which are usually shy and rarely move far from woodland cover, were frequent visitors. One day a water rail, a secretive wading bird, more often heard than seen, was rehomed in Lowes' reed beds. It had been found in a town east of Dunkeld, in a garage, and nurtured until it was strong enough to be released. The reed beds at Lowes already supported water rail and gave the small bird its best chance of survival. The appearance on the loch of a pintail duck – a long-necked, small-headed species, slightly bigger than a mallard – was a welcome surprise, never before seen at Lowes.

Just before Christmas the snow that fell on the iced-over loch created a magical world – although few birds were visible. From among the ever-elusive water rails, one emerged near to the visitor centre, forced out of the reed beds by the big freeze to feed; staff scattered mealworms on the ground outside the centre to help it. There were red squirrels about, with a baby one, a kit, appearing most days. A fallow-deer antler was added to the reserve's feeding zone, for the squirrels to gnaw as a supplement to their peanut diet, which, alone, could lead to calcium deficiency.

January brought harsh weather with temperatures on a few nights down to −17°C. The loch was still covered with a thick sheet of ice. Thousands of miles further south, however, after a successful autumn migration, Lady was enjoying the subtropics, with plentiful fish, in West Africa's coastal mangrove forests and broad rivers. There she and other migratory ospreys could rest during a relatively sedentary period in their yearly cycle. At Lowes, though, the birds were struggling. The unusual sighting at a reserve bird feeder of a reed bunting showed that the extreme weather was making life tough for birds. The Lowes feeders were already well used by many species – a few robins and bramblings, a handful of pheasants and hundreds of chaffinches.

By February, not much wildlife was evident at Lowes, where the loch remained frozen. Around any tiny pockets of water, ducks congregated. A few adventurous mallards, the most recognizable, archetypal duck, could be seen sliding around on the ice. The males had already begun their mating displays, shaking their heads with their breasts held clear of the water, their necks outstretched, and doing the tail-shake too, as they pursued the females. But the females voted with their feet, not in the least interested in those freezing conditions. Reserve staff had installed artificial goldeneye duck nest boxes, some twelve feet off the ground, the height goldeneye prefer for their nests – forward planning for when the fancy took them in the spring.

Greylag geese were arriving, thousands amassing at sunset, and the discovery of three widgeon, many of which visit the UK in winter from Iceland, Scandinavia and Russia, was a happy one. This duck's distinctive white belly, visible in flight, had so far that year been noticeable only by its absence; its appearance was a sign that perhaps the big freeze might soon be over.

Spring would come and with it the osprey. Would Lady return in 2010? Like other ospreys programmed to breed, Lady's spring migration started each year in late February or early March. Instinct had always brought her back to Lowes towards the end of March. If she survived the arduous return migration from West Africa to breed successfully it would be her twentieth consecutive year of raising young at the Loch of the Lowes reserve.

The end of March was also when that season's new Perthshire ranger was due to arrive at Lowes. In 2010 Emma Rawling, who had responsibility for seven of the Scottish Wildlife Trust's reserves, would take over. Her background is in veterinary nursing and animal welfare.

She had done a great deal of bird rescue and looked after injured buzzards and sparrowhawks, as well as foreign raptors, or birds of prey, in Australia, where she comes from. Rawling is passionate about the osprey and interested scientifically in its reintroduction to its once native territories. She was keen to do whatever she could to help rare or once-extinct species regain a foothold in their ancestral lands. The Lowes' job would offer her the chance to put her ideas into practice. Her arrival, as part of the expert osprey team already in place at Lowes, was expected to coincide with Lady's imminent return.

2 Return of the Fisher King

Whether or not Lady would come back to Lowes that spring, ospreys as a species were returning to Scotland, the UK and many of their breeding grounds around the world, ever more arriving each nesting season. For a very long time, however, this had not been so, which is evident from the osprey's amber listing in the conservationists' traffic-light system – red, amber, green – that signals increasing degrees of conservation concern. There was sound reason for adding the osprey to any list of species at risk: it had been persecuted by humans for centuries and, if not wiped out, the few nesting birds that were left had at one stage effectively deserted British shores. It was a story repeated across Europe.

The harsh reality is that, until its return in the 1950s, the osprey was last recorded as a breeding bird in the UK in Scotland in 1916, only appearing thereafter in British skies as a passage migrant. It had died out earlier, about the 1840s, in England (where a last nesting pair is variously claimed in Gloucestershire and Somerset), possibly during the nineteenth century in Ireland and even earlier in Wales (where it is likely that the birds were extinct before official ornithological records began). It is known, although no records were kept, that historically ospreys had nested throughout the UK, from Scotland to Cornwall, and there were plenty of them, probably in the region of seven thousand pairs. No one knows for sure when the osprey stopped coming to the UK to breed – if, indeed, that was what they did.

For some who live among the osprey, such as Peter Ferns, Loch of the Lowes' visitor-centre manager, who has watched the birds – and Lady especially – for many springs and summers as breeding pairs, the osprey was never extinct in Scotland. He believes that they never left Scottish forests and waters, although they were scarce. He recalls that his grandfather, born in 1910, used to remark that there were always ospreys in Perthshire when he was growing up. The reality is that, during the period of their supposed extinction, the Great Depression and two world wars were of more interest to most people than birds.

What the experts do agree on, including eminent osprey authority and Scottish naturalist Roy Dennis, is that by the end of the eighteenth century the osprey had become rare in the British Isles. In the third edition (1927) of their *Manual of British Birds*, which includes details of 500 birds (there were 384 in the 1899 edition), Howard Saunders and W. Eagle Clarke describe the osprey as 'formerly a summer visitant; now a rare passage migrant'. They explain how, traditionally, ospreys had bred widely in Britain, even on England's south coast and in the Lake District, until the end of the eighteenth century. Thereafter the Highland lochs were the breeding ospreys' final UK refuge. Since the 1899 edition of the handbook, the bird the authors describe as 'one of the most interesting of our native avifauna' had been 'exterminated in its last British haunts'. How had this tragedy befallen the osprey?

Ospreys were once found virtually throughout the world. Alan Poole, based at the Cornell Laboratory of Ornithology in New York State, has spent many years studying them in southern New England and Florida Bay. In his book *Ospreys: A Natural and Unnatural History*, he describes ospreys similar to those that exist today as 'well established in much of their current breeding range at about the same time our earliest ape-like ancestors left forests and began to walk upright across the plains of Africa'. Another classic osprey text, Philip Brown and George Waterston's *The Return of the Osprey*, mentions a reference to them in Aristotle's *Natural History*, and points out that Shakespeare and the Elizabethans were familiar with birds of prey through falconry (and that falconers may even have trained ospreys). James IV of Scotland reputedly had ospreys taught to catch fish; James VI – James I after the Union of

Scotland with England – is said to have kept them on the Thames at Westminster, with cormorants and otters. Any notion of training osprey is largely discredited, because it is generally accepted that the birds do not thrive in captivity and would not have accepted life as trained hunters because of their intransigence and the fact that they know who they are.

Ospreys are mentioned in the last of Shakespeare's tragic plays, *Coriolanus*, probably written in 1607–8: 'I think he'll be to Rome/As is the osprey to the fish, who takes it/By sovereignty of nature.' These lines, endowing the legendary hero Coriolanus with the ospreys' fisher-king nature, tapped into the medieval belief that the birds mesmerized their prey; that they were merciless warrior-birds before which the hapless fish keeled over. Ospreys eat fresh fish, almost exclusively, and without it they would die; it comes as little surprise that they are such accomplished hunters. Four hundred years after Shakespeare wrote those lines, tribal fishermen in Senegal canoe the surf to their fishing nets singing the praises of the osprey's hunting skills. They have been known to carry with them, as a talisman, the bones of a fish caught by an osprey.

Ospreys are magical and compelling, the swashbucklers of the bird world; they entrance anyone fortunate enough to see them with their spectacular fishing skills and masterly powers of flight. They are an alluring bird: beautiful, inspiring, elegant, huge. Today they are popular but, like the eagle, falcon and other raptors, this was not always so: they have been hunted and shot, poisoned or trapped, their nests robbed of eggs and their food sources diminished or polluted. To the Irish poet William Butler Yeats, in his epic *The wanderings of Oisin* (1889), the osprey is a mourning lament: 'Nor the grey wandering osprey Sorrow'. By the end of the eighteenth century this magnificent bird, esteemed, feared and loved, had been largely exiled from British lands. A bird that had once spent all its springs and summers nesting on British shores and inland waters had gone.

This was surprising in a bird that is known to be intensely territorial about its landscapes, whose specific places – where it hatches, fledges, fishes, breeds and raises its young – are firmly imprinted in it. The osprey has a strong sense of place, which David Gessner describes, in his acclaimed *Return of the Osprey: A Season of Flight and Wonder*, as an almost unfailing internal compass that directs it back, powering an unerring loyalty, to where it came from. A wealth of stories exists about how ospreys build their nests repeatedly in unsuitable or incongruous places, atop once derelict houses or on power lines or pylons, and are then slaughtered for their determination to remain where instinct, unalterable genetic law, tells them they belong.

More than that, ospreys are not known as 'scaredy-birds', shy or timid as, say, the who-can-hide-better-than-a-bittern, which nests out of sight tucked away in reed beds, or the albatross that inhabits some of the remotest corners of the world. The osprey is bold. But still they disappeared. The osprey's vanishing was not just about a loss of habitat, which is, of course, a major threat for wild animals the world over. Despite its unrelenting fight to retain its place, it had a fight on its hands to virtual extinction, which, over the centuries, had forced its retreat to remote fastnesses, seeking refuge far from human persecution – from hunters and trappers, from being poisoned or shot.

Some say that it was competition for fish that fixed the osprey's fate. As a fish-eating raptor, it is unique among birds of prey. In the Middle Ages it was hunted to stop it raiding stew ponds, the vast reservoirs of fish that belonged, in the main, to landed estates and monasteries. For anyone wealthy enough, the stew ponds, regularly restocked, were a source of fine and varied dining. In mid-sixteenth-century London, a Great Pike Garden existed at Bankside, opposite St Paul's Cathedral; pike and other stew-pond fish were enjoyed by humans and raided by ospreys, which did not help the bird's popularity.

During the seventeenth and early eighteenth centuries, persecution by hunters, gamekeepers, egg and skin collectors contributed to the osprey's scarcity in Britain. By the time it was being mentioned in natural-history books, its numbers were in steep decline, so much so that by the mid-1800s it had been almost wiped out, except in Scotland. It was not long before it had vanished from Scottish lochs and shores too: the birds and their eggs had become collectors' top trophies. In a cruel twist, it was the osprey's ever increasing rarity that made it even more of a target for egg and skin collectors.

As early as 1825, the Scottish ornithologist P. J. Selby recorded that the nests about Loch Awe, known as the Jewel of Argyll, were 'generally robbed when containing eggs, and the young are hardly ever permitted to escape'. Just a few years later, in 1833, he reported 'the young were hardly ever permitted to fly'. In 1832, the Scottish naturalist Sir William Jardine described how an osprey pair or even two breeding pairs could often be found around many Highland lochs; by 1860, there were at least two osprey pairs in Galloway, but so rapid was their extermination that, according to Saunders and Eagle Clarke, by the end of the nineteenth century 'only two eyries were known to be tenanted – both in Inverness-shire, and the last of these was deserted in 1911'.

It was the Victorians who finally did it for the birds, given the zeal with which they dispatched so much wildlife. Their imperialism encompassed the animal kingdom as well as distant lands. In the nineteenth and early twentieth centuries the birds suffered intense persecution by egg and skin collectors, who sometimes collected to order for profit, but were mainly obsessed with amassing them for display in their own grand houses. Ospreys were shot routinely by fishermen and gamekeepers, with scant regard for conservation, in accordance with the endemic practice of eliminating predators of game on sporting estates – the birds were perceived as eating, literally, into the estate profits. Deforestation to create the heathland ideal for raising game birds destroyed their habitat, including the trees in which they liked to nest. The birds were not difficult targets during the breeding season: they would circle their nests defensively at the approach of any potential predator and were picked off with ease by renowned nineteenth-century sportsmen such as William Dunbar and Charles St John. Of his egg- and skin-collecting forays in 1848–9 in Sutherland, in the northern Highlands, Dunbar himself wrote in 1850, in a letter to English egg collector John Wolley: 'I am afraid that Mr St John, yourself, and your humble servant, have finally done for the ospreys.'

Nonetheless there are other published accounts of breeding. Until 1908, an osprey eyrie was found in an oak tree on an island at the east end of Loch Arkaig – one of the many east–west lochs the glaciers scoured out across the western Highlands during the last Ice Age – and there is general consensus, not supported by anything written or published, that a pair nested at nearby Loch Loyne in 1916. If rumour is at all reliable, in an echo of Peter Ferns's grandfather, a pair nested in the Highlands in 1926. Later, in a Rewards Scheme set up in 1949 by the Royal Society for the Protection of Birds (RSPB), a prize was offered to anyone able to verify that young had flown from the nests of several rare species, including the golden eagle, hen harrier, marsh harrier, avocet, spoonbill, black tern, red kite, white-tailed eagle, honey buzzard, golden oriole, hoopoe – and osprey.

But if the final straw for many birds was Victorian killing and collecting sprees, it was in that era, too, that the seeds of redemption were sown. February 1889 saw the creation, in Didsbury, Manchester, of an early form of what became the RSPB. There had been an initiative earlier in the century, sparked by the destruction of native sea birds, such as great crested grebes and kittiwakes, which had led to the Sea Birds Preservation Act 1869 and the Wild Birds Protection Act 1880. But the spur to the formation of the new society was the ruthless global destruction of birds with ever more exotic plumes suitable for millinery fashions and ceremonial dress. The Society's aim was for women – and in its earliest days it consisted entirely of women – to stand firm against the cruelty of plume-wearing, which involved the widespread killing of birds for their feathers. In 1891, the Didsbury group and the ladies who attended a Mrs Phillips's Fur and Feather meetings in Croydon, south London, joined forces as the Society for the Protection of Birds.

In October of that year, the Society's initial report appeared, with one of its first publications: 'The Osprey, or Egrets and Aigrettes. Leaflet no. 1 = Destruction of Ornamental Plumaged Birds'. It was a protest against feathers in hats, by author, naturalist and ornithologist William Henry Hudson, a prominent and persuasive voice in early bird conservation. Two years later, he wrote a further protest to *The Times*, to which the paper responded in its leader: 'How long will women tolerate a fashion which involves so wanton, wholesale, and hideous cruelty as this? ... Let it be clearly understood, once and for all, that a feathered woman is a cruel woman.'

Four years later, Hudson featured in *The Times* again, writing this time not only against the wearing of 'ospreys' but of all the birds whose skins and feathers were 'on view in the dusty desert of the show-rooms in Houndsditch [in the City of London]'. *The Times* replied with another leading article. 'Osprey feathers' were, in this instance, mostly those of the heron species, the egret; in his section on natural history in *The Return of the Osprey*, George Waterston, one-time director of the RSPB in Scotland, explains that 'osprey, so curiously applied, is probably a corruption of the French word *esprit*, by which these feathers were known in the time of the German naturalist Pallas (1741–1811)'.

In September 1899, Queen Victoria confirmed that certain regiments would stop wearing 'osprey' plumes, only to replace them with ostrich feathers. In the dress of the Viceroy of India's Bodyguard, turbans had been sub-stituted for plumed caps. However, it was women's fashion that had been responsible for the annual slaughter of white egrets and herons during the nesting season, at which time the birds were in full plumage. And it was women who were now fighting against it. Among the Society for the Protection of Birds' most stalwart supporters were those who might once have worn plumes, such as the Duchess of Portland, who had become its first president in 1891. Other significant figures included the then leading orni-thologist Professor Alfred Newton, who gave his support to a cause that quickly gained in popularity and widened its objectives. In 1904, just fifteen years after the Society had been founded, it was granted its Royal Charter.

In 1908, the Importation of Plumage (Prohibition) Bill was introduced to Parliament, although it was not passed until 1921. In the meantime, the RSPB, based in Kensington's Queen's Anne Gate, had published *Feathers and Facts . . . A reply to the feather-trade and review of facts with reference to the persecution of birds for their plumage*. It was concerned with the trade in birds and their feathers for millinery use and the destruction of wild-bird life by plume-hunters, and included a chapter on artificial 'ospreys'. Its findings were supported, it said, by like-minded societies in Europe, North and South America, India and other parts of the world.

Further help came in 1954 with the Protection of Birds Act, which included general amendments to bird-protection legislation that included enhanced safety for the osprey and its eggs at all times via new penalties. But half a century on ospreys remain under threat, although not so much for the beauty of their feathers. Today the bird is threatened by egg collectors, a peculiarly British phenomenon, and illegal killing. The Wildlife and Countryside Act 1981 makes it an offence to take intentionally, injure or kill an osprey or to take, damage or destroy its nest, eggs or young. It is also an offence to disturb intentionally or recklessly the birds close to their nest during the breeding season (which can happen, unwittingly, in the search for a perfect photo).

Breaking the law can lead to fines of up to £5,000 per offence and/or a prison sentence of up to six months. Nevertheless, to Peter Ferns's knowledge – and he is not alone in saying this – ospreys are still persecuted, despite their legal protection, in parts of the UK. They are often found shot. In late 2010, for instance, the RSPB offered a £1,000 reward for information about the shooting of a young osprey in Lincolnshire. The bird, which had been tagged in Sweden and was only eighty-six days old, was found near a fish farm at Hundon Manor, Caister. Veterinary tests revealed that it had been shot twice.

Thankfully, today, many landowners, farmers, game-keepers and gillies do not mind ospreys on their land; indeed, more likely, they see their presence as a privilege. That has greatly helped the osprey. One gillie, who runs a huge stretch of the River Tay with several ospreys nesting on his beat, looks after every one of them, ensuring nobody approaches them.

In Scotland, osprey survival is further assisted by the Nature Conservation (Scotland) Act 2004, which has widened the legal parameters of the birds' protection. Perhaps fittingly, given that breeding ospreys were last officially recorded in the UK in Scotland in 1916, it was the Scottish Highlands that saw the first returning pair of breeding ospreys. Off the record, an osprey pair was said to have bred there successfully in 1954, rearing two young. In any case, the 1950s saw the osprey start to re-colonize the UK, perhaps through birds of Scandinavian origin.

It was to the ancient Caledonian pine forest at the RSPB's Loch Garten, Abernethy Forest wildlife reserve, near Aviemore, in Strathspey, that the birds chose to return in 1959. Its relative abundance of forest trees in which to nest, and its freshwater lochs, rivers, estuaries and fish-farms, from which to feed, made this an ideal breeding site. An osprey pair has nested at Loch Garten every year since, a succession of breeding pairs going on to raise more than eighty young. That year, an osprey observation hide was opened to the public, attracting thousands of visitors. It was a radical move to invite people in, but one that paid off. The RSPB Osprey Centre has become one of the world's most famous conservation sites, featuring other rare species, among them capercaillie, crested tit, goldeneye and Scottish crossbill. From small beginnings, the osprey's return to Scotland's wild places is now hailed as a significant milestone for the birds and a miracle for early conservationists.

Continued recolonization in Britain from the 1950s was slow. To begin with, it was a while before the 1954 law used any of its teeth. In autumn 1960, for instance, a young female osprey, possibly one of only two to be reared in the UK that summer, was shot in southern England, where it had paused, presumably, to build up its strength for its migration to Africa. The man responsible was prosecuted but received a derisory £10 fine that came nowhere near matching the real cost of the loss.

Over time, however, statistics began to show a more

cheering story: by 1976, there were fourteen breeding osprey pairs in Scotland; fifteen years later, in 1981, this had increased to seventy-one; by 2001, there were 158 pairs in the UK, still mainly in Scotland, although by then in England too. That same year an osprey pair on Rutland Water raised the first English osprey chick in almost a century and a half, following the translocation of sixty-four Scottish ospreys to the reservoir between 1996 and 2001. Subsequently there were also nests in Cumbria and Northumbria.

By 2010, about two hundred osprey pairs were breeding in Scotland. The UK-wide tally – with ospreys having returned to breed in Wales for the first time in 2004 – added up to a possible grand total of 220 pairs. Their numbers were watched worldwide by nature lovers and conservationists, whose interest in and support for the birds was ever growing. In many parts of the world, osprey reintroduction and translocation programmes, like those in Britain and North America, were attracting interest from Europe to Japan and the Middle East.

So, when it comes to breeding numbers there is good reason for optimism, but here's the rub. While two hundred or so osprey pairs may sound like, and is, a great start, given that in 1959 the dial was set at zero, it is only a start, still not sufficient to remove the species from its amber listing as a bird of conservation concern. Crucially, the number is not enough for adequate genetic diversity: one disease could wipe out the entire recolonization.

In autumn 2010 the eleventh in the series of annual reports that summarize the fortunes of UK bird populations, 'The State of the UK's Birds 2010', was published. As 2010 was the International Year of Biodiversity, the report examined the efficacy of efforts to conserve the UK's birdlife since the global Convention on Biological Diversity came into force in 1993. It came out as the Nagoya Biodiversity Summit in Japan reviewed attempts to protect wildlife and showed that the number of endangered bird species in the UK had increased. The UK has not met its targets to halt or even slow the loss of wild birds, despite successful efforts to bring back some species from the brink. Conservationists say that birds still need help to increase their population.

And, according to other reports that autumn, conservation experts warned that the world is in the increasingly tight grip of the 'sixth great extinction': imported species and diseases, hunting and the destruction of natural habitats are dealing fatal blows to indigenous plants and animals. The International Union for the Conservation of Nature (IUCN) compiles the world's official lists of threatened species. The osprey, with its extremely large range worldwide and significant population increase in the last forty years, is of least concern on the IUCN red list. But the bird is listed as threatened, endangered or a species of special concern in several US states and protected under the US Migratory Bird Act. In the UK and Europe, as published in *Birds of Conservation Concern 3*

(2009), the more than one hundred amber-listed birds included the nightingale, puffin, kittiwake, Arctic tern, curlew, golden eagle, red kite and marsh harrier, alongside the osprey.

3 Lady at the Loch

In April 1969, just two weeks after the Scottish Wildlife Trust had purchased Loch of the Lowes as a nature reserve, a pair of breeding ospreys arrived. It was a decade since the first birds had returned to Scotland to nest and, clearly, the UK's ospreys return had continued. At the time of their arrival, the birds at Lowes were only the fifth known breeding pair to have arrived in the UK since 1916.

With its tranquil loch, full of fish, and remote setting amid suitable tall, flat-topped nesting trees, Lowes was an ideal locale for ospreys. The birds balance their lives between land and water, occupying nests usually no more than two or three miles from lake, river or ocean (although, if they have to, they will fly up to eight miles to hunt). The following year, 1970, the new breeding pair at Lowes laid a clutch of eggs in a brand-new nest. Ospreys usually do not start breeding until they are between three and five years old. They may build a nest in the first year but do not lay eggs. Or they may produce eggs that fail to hatch. That year all looked good, until a fierce May storm wrecked nest and eggs, a cruel blow for the birds and the conservationists.

The early 1970s were a precarious period for Scotland's breeding ospreys. At the decade's start, it was clear that they needed encouragement to regain their foothold in old territories. The first pair that came back to Scotland, to Loch Garten, did so of their own accord, probably as an overflow of the Scandinavian population. But they had needed a lot of help to turn into ten, twenty, thirty, forty pairs. Ospreys have never been reintroduced, strictly speaking, but they have been recolonized (and translocated as, years later, the Rutland Water ospreys had been). It is more difficult to re-colonize them than, say, red kites, another major UK conservation success story. The red kite is a carrion-eater and can be fed butcher's scraps to ensure its survival. A regular supply of live fish for the osprey is a different matter. The most conservationists can do for the osprey is to provide nesting platforms and protect nests. Providing nest sites is much easier and more effective than providing food.

After the terrible storm of 1970, the Lowes pair needed to be given the right nesting conditions and support. The Scottish Wildlife Trust built an osprey eyrie at Lowes in the event of the birds' return the next spring. Happily, the ospreys showed no inclination to give up, and their new nest must have passed muster because, in 1971, the pair tailored it to fit, and after a happy courtship, the female laid eggs, which eventually hatched.

The Trust's handiwork was home to the first two osprey chicks to fledge at Lowes in decades. The new family was protected with twenty-four-hour observation by Lowes staff and a local volunteer army of bird lovers. Lowes decided to open the osprey nest to public view, much as had happened at Loch Garten. By 1992, ospreys had success-fully reared their young on that nest in more than half of the breeding years since their return in 1969. Lady's presence was part and parcel of that continued success: it proved that the osprey was enjoying a new lease of life in the UK.

Lady first arrived at Lowes in spring 1991. Peter Ferns believes that she is from Scotland, from Perthshire itself. His confidence in saying this stems partly from the knowledge that female ospreys tend to return to their original nest site – to where they fledged or first flew the nest (this tendency is known as philopatry). If Lady had been a male bird, he would have been doubly sure, because male ospreys return more reliably to within a roughly twenty-five-mile radius. Female birds tend to venture a little further. If Lady wasn't from Perthshire, she was most likely from Sweden. Whether from Scotland or Sweden, she would have migrated to West Africa for her first winter, remaining there for two, three or four years.

On her first return north to breed, Lady would have been attracted by a lone male osprey that had laid a claim to the

Lowes nest and would have been busy lining it, ever hopeful of sharing it with a new partner. With his strong instinct to breed, he knew exactly how to court her and persuade her to stay.

The first weapon in the male osprey's arsenal is his glorious sky dance or fish flight, a courtship display more atmospheric and stirring than any of the slap, sequins or razzmatazz of the Moulin Rouge. When the species was rare in Scotland during the 1960s and 1970s, these amazing aerial shows, performed mostly by single males early in courtship, were a main event in the osprey breeding season. If mating and feeding are the bread-and-butter basics of osprey courtship, the sky dance is the caviar and champagne, an osprey spring spectacular that aims to turn a girl's head.

The sky dance is the lone male osprey's big chance to woo his intended – as well as to mark out his territory. He aims to show the female bird that he has what it takes, that he is a good catch in every sense – he often performs with a fish in his talons. The dance, executed above the nesting ground, is an exhilarating extravaganza worthy of the Red Devils, a stunning sequence of dramatic sky dives, in which the bird falls steeply for a hundred feet or more, and tantalizing check reversals, when he pulls out of the dive and rises again, wings beating rapidly to regain height, fish booty dangling enticingly. Another brief wing-beating hover, then an abrupt swoop down a hundred feet, treading air, then rising once more astonishingly quickly.

This stage of osprey courtship is anything but subtle, but it is great theatre. It does what it says on the tin: it gets girls and nests, and comes with an unmistakable soundtrack. As Alan F. Poole says, 'No natural sound is more characteristic of osprey country than the rhythmic, penetrating *eeeet-eeeet-eeeet* of displaying males.' That cry announces the start of the breeding season.

It would have been the Lowes nest, ownership secured by an alluring available male, that clinched it for Lady. A good nest site is key to breeding success and can endure for generations; Lady had shown discrimination and found herself a good one. Ospreys are mostly monogamous, in that they form a pair bond, one male mating with one female. It is the same for 90 per cent of bird species, although a bond may last for a single nesting (American house wrens), an entire breeding season (most birds, including the majority of passerines, or perching birds, such as crows, finches and thrushes), several successive breeding seasons (American robins, tree swallows, mourning doves) or life (albatrosses, petrels, swans, geese, eagles, some owls and parrots – and ospreys). Don't confuse monogamy with romance: for the osprey, mating for life is all about preservation of the species.

Although ospreys pair for life, they are as much attached to their nests, to the familiar ground that they stake out and claim, as they are to each other. They are known to defend their nests fiercely, sometimes to the death. Once they have established ownership, most adult ospreys return to breed in the same nest year after year. If ospreys survive to adulthood, older birds especially tend to remain faithful to their mate unless, as in Lady's experience in spring 2010 (and, earlier, in 1996), the mate does not return and a new partner is found.

Exceptions to the rule include 1976, when sexual experimentation reached Lowes, and monogamy was abandoned for polygyny: a male osprey mated with two females, which both went on to lay eggs on the same nest. The experiment was not a success – no young hatched.

For all sorts of reasons, the possibility of failure could never be ruled out. The osprey had not been breeding at Lowes for long – just a couple of decades – when Lady had first appeared. In 1991, she arrived at Lowes, found herself a mate and sealed the bond with a nest; her first breeding season at Lowes had begun. She must have got it right because breeding was successful.

The joy of Lady's arrival was tempered by concern because it heralded other arrivals. Egg thieves were extremely active at that time and would instantly appear at any nest site once a bird was known to be incubating eggs there. Lady's nest and eggs would have been especially prized, as ospreys were so rare in the early 1990s, which presented the two staff who were running the Lowes reserve with a problem: they did not have the resources for a twenty-four-hour osprey watch, without which the nest was vulnerable to human predation. What to do?

Why not call in the army? The Gordon Highlanders were approached and responded in good spirit, their presence bolstered by the British Army's expensive night-sight surveillance equipment. With some extra help from local people, known to Lowes staff and trusted by them, who did shifts as volunteer guardians, Lady and her eggs were kept safe that year – and have been ever since.

In summer 2010, a blog-poster called Nuphar, who had been at Lowes in 1991 and had a long association with the reserve, posted her memories of Lady's first year on the Lowes osprey blog. She described how, during that first egg watch, the regiment's brigadier had come down 'from Inverness with his entourage, kilts a-swinging, to see what his Gordon Highlanders had volunteered to give up their leave to protect . . . The osprey put on a really good show for him, seven of them circling in the sky and the male doing his darnedest to send them packing.' Nuphar could never fathom whence those seven birds sprang, but their timing was immaculate, and their sky-high jinks sent the brigadier home happy.

Mission accomplished for Lady too. She left Lowes at the end of the breeding season, and her return migration to West Africa would have been a solo long-haul flight. After an intense four or five months constantly in each other's company, male and female osprey might not see each other again until the following year. The next spring, if fortunate, they would return to their nesting site for another round of breeding.

Lady returned on 7 April the following year, and her time

at Lowes that spring and summer was recorded by reserve ranger Dave Allan. She arrived six days after her mate; male birds tend to turn up a few days ahead of the females, although not reliably so – more experienced older breeders, male or female, may get back ahead of younger birds who fly in sometimes weeks later. It was in 1995 that Lady was first at Lowes, spotted at just after nine a.m. on 1 April. Her presence was confirmed later that day when she was seen posting a No Vacancies sign above the eyrie by circling the site and calling continuously to establish her territory. The nest would be hers for the season, although she might have appreciated some help in defending her claim on it. As her cries continued to be heard over the loch, a slow whistling *kew-kew-kew*, the call an osprey often makes when other ospreys are near, she could be heard up to half a mile away. But it was likely that she was calling to her mate, trying to establish whether he was close by and able to assist her, or still miles distant on his long, fraught journey.

Left alone to defend her nest, perhaps she wondered if her mate would make a successful return trip to Lowes. Migration, that wonder of the natural world, comes with no guarantees: only around 37 out of 100 ospreys flying to Africa in their first migration will come back three or four years later. Birds migrate to survive but sometimes their perilous journey from north to south, or vice versa, kills them. Ospreys, like other migrating birds, sometimes get lost or die when they run into bad weather, especially heavy rainstorms, thick fog or mist. Then the best option for the birds is to fly downwind and trust to make landfall, feed there to rebuild their strength and eventually resume their migration; a few lucky ones will weather a major storm.

Migrants face a raft of difficulties, as satellite-tracked birds show, especially juveniles on first migration. They tend to follow the same routes each year – as, again, satellite-tracked birds have shown – and get better at it as they get older, no longer solely dependent on their genetic intelligence. Like humans, the more they do something, the better at it they become.

Lady was testament to this, yet her exact route, what she did and where she went, will never be known for sure because she was never ringed or tagged. Where she came from or what she did for the six months of every year after she had flown from Lowes in search of the African sun, for a spell of perching, staring and building strength for next year's northern migration and breeding months, will always remain a mystery.

Most likely, she would have reached West Africa in September, then spent the other half of her year in its lakes, marshes and mangrove swamps, its rivers and their estuaries, or along the Atlantic coasts from Mauritania to Guinea and inland to Mali. The West African wetlands and large river estuaries would probably have been her winter habitat from September to February. More easterly breeders, such as ospreys that nest in Finland, would overwinter in Nigeria or East Africa or even, occasionally, in South Africa.

Why Lady was never ringed is a mystery too. More than thirty-six million birds have been ringed in the UK in the last hundred years to make it easier to identify them and help with their conservation. In the early days of the osprey's return to Scotland, conservation was not overly scientific so no one had ringed Lady. Conservation practice has come a long way since, and advances such as satellite tagging are a potentially exciting breakthrough in unravelling nature's mysteries, especially the intricate detail of long-distance bird migration. To the birds, it is what they do; to everyone else it is a miracle.

Lady had migrated many times and come a long way in more senses than one. Her species had risen phoenix-like from the ashes of their extinction, dismissing the gloom of their regretted demise, to return to the United States, Europe and Scotland – to Perthshire and Loch of the Lowes – as an emblem of international bird conservation and an encouraging example of how it is sometimes possible to triumph over adversity. Her time at Lowes had only just begun.

4 The wonders of spring

Typically, says Fiona Hutton, assistant visitor-centre manager at Lowes, she was off duty on 23 March 2010 when Lady returned. It was a day when they had experienced problems with the nest camera and wanted verification that the bird they had sighted was Lady, The reserve office rang Hutton at home, and she went in to work to double-check. It was definitely Lady: she has very individual markings so, for anyone watching her day after day, it was like identifying an old friend.

The Lowes reserve had been anticipating the return of its usual pair of breeding ospreys, Lady and Eric, and had even offered a prize set of binoculars to the first person to spot them. Who would be the first to glimpse, in the distance, the gleam of their distinctive white breast feathers or the flash of their white heads? Who would spot them first, flying in on their long, narrow wings, white beneath and marked with brown, their tails barred brown and buff (the male's generally paler)? When they got closer, it would be easy to distinguish any juvenile bird, its upper parts layered with overlapping creamy-tipped brown feathers and the wonderful orange eyes that set them apart from the adult birds.

Almost like fingerprints, a bird's feather markings are unique and distinctive. The key marks for establishing who's who among ospreys are on the head, especially the dark patterning on the crown and the Zorro-like eye band – the variable colour above and below the birds' eyes. For Peter Ferns, the clear Y-shape in the feathers on top of Lady's head was most distinctive. Via the Lowes high-definition camera, he could also zoom in on the highly distinctive marking on Lady's right eye, almost like a tiny teardrop seeping out below the iris. To him, Lady was as recognizable as any friend or neighbour. He had been watching her for so many years that he could identify her almost instantly: to him, no two ospreys looked alike.

It is the same for anyone who watches the birds regularly. Roy Dennis supervises, among other osprey enterprises, a nest in Speyside. When he goes into the field he can recognize which bird he is looking at, not just because of the coloured leg rings, but also because of its markings, its personalized feather tattoos. To Lowes ranger Dave Allan, observing Lady in 1992, her most distinguishing feature was her dark upper breast, in contrast to the male osprey's pure white. Everyone had their own means of telling them apart.

Size was helpful too: as Dave Allan recorded in his notes, Lady was marginally bigger than her mate, which is the general rule. Females tend to be heavier than males, their wings are longer, as are their tails, claws and bills, a tendency known as reversed sexual dimorphism. What is surprising, however, is that although the osprey look like big birds – which indeed they are, with their five-foot wingspan and the equivalent size of a buzzard or a small eagle – they weigh less than the average family cat, about four pounds, the male birds sometimes less.

By 22 March, the loch at Lowes was finally free of ice, not only enabling ospreys better to fish from it but also signalling a change in the seasons. Now spring had sprung, the reserve would soon be alive with birdsong as the birds competed for territories and mates. The approaching wonders of spring ushered in the new season's residents. That day the year's first swallow was seen near the hides (like the osprey, an amber-listed bird, but one famous for spending most of its life on the wing), and romance blossomed for the great crested grebe, an elegant waterbird with the ornate head plumes that had once led to it being hunted. The grebes' courtship displays, in which they performed their bill-touching, neck-swaying, head-shaking breeding dance, were extraordinarily elaborate and a joy to watch. All the birds were putting on a show, some more comical than beautiful, with swans and goldeneye ducks taking their turn. The goldeneyes are a diving duck, another amber-listed bird, which first nested in Scotland in 1970 and since then has been enticed to nest in the specially designed boxes twelve feet above the water.

The biggest news, however, was the season's first osprey, seen at some point the previous weekend, 20 and 21 March, on the vernal equinox that marked spring's official start. Disappointingly, it was neither Lady nor Eric but a passage bird, one that stays only a short time in an area, possibly on its seasonal migration route. That Saturday, an un-ringed osprey visited the Lowes osprey nest and was seen at the loch on the Sunday, too, but it quickly moved on.

A day or so later there was no doubt: feathers, markings, colouring and size helped Hutton to identify the newly arrived female osprey soaring above her as Lady. She felt a thrill of excitement that the osprey had come back. It had been a case of wait and see ever since Lady's departure the previous August. For the adult birds, migrations in spring tend to be speedier than those made in the autumn: they are determined to get back fast to give themselves the best chance of reclaiming their mate and nest. For a few years, Lady had arrived at Lowes by late March or early April; now she had done so again.

Lady was no longer young: she had lived twice as long as most other ospreys and, in that sense, she was existing on borrowed time. The Lowes osprey team greeted her arrival with delight and astonishment at her extraordinary tenacity and stubborn endurance, but their pleasure at her return was qualified by the fear that she might not be able to secure her nest and breed that year. She had survived the hazardous spring migration from West Africa to Lowes, and she looked in good shape, a without-which-nothing requirement for the breeding season. All this was positive, but the season had to progress one step at a time, and the next step was for Lady's breeding partner of fourteen years, the regular resident male of the Lowes osprey partnership, Eric, to show up. He was expected back at any moment and would be instantly identifiable by his green leg ring when he arrived.

But there was no sign of him. Reports had come in of bad weather, desert dust storms on the migration route, which could follow the coast northwards but also crossed the huge waterless stretches of the Sahara from Mauritania, Senegal and the Gambia, before soaring above the Atlas Mountains of North Africa, heading for Europe, sometimes via Gibraltar. The adverse weather conditions might have slowed him, and his presence was required: there had already been a stray male osprey hanging around the loch calling. It had twice tried to land on Lady's nest but she had seen it off swiftly and fiercely. Once Eric arrived, he would chase away any rogue males or floaters, unattached ospreys looking for nest sites, and other intruders, helping Lady to secure the nest.

That year in particular, the birds' arrival in good physical health and a secure nest would be just the start: for the osprey season to be truly successful, there must be eggs, chicks and successful fledging. Lady's great age and Eric's no show made this much less than a racing certainty. A hint of fragility threatened Lady and Eric's long and unbroken series of winning breeding seasons. Someone, one day, would call time.

Lady was waiting for Eric that year because he was her regular mate – commonly known as 'Stressed Eric' to Lowes osprey bloggers because they thought she stressed him out. The pair had been together since 1996, the year her first mate at Lowes had not returned. Lady and Eric were an established couple, who had an arrangement that worked: they knew their roles and exactly what they were meant to do each year. Lady often returned first to the nest and, because they had been together so long, needed no alluring sky-dance courtship.

As she awaited Eric's arrival, other male ospreys put on a bit of a show, no sky dance but making it clear that they wanted her to give them a chance. Sometimes they flew around the nest and came too close, trying to land and mate. She waited throughout late March into the first few days of April, spending much of her time on a high perch to one side of the nest from where she kept watch, like a sailor's wife scanning an endless, empty horizon.

As she waited, Lady kept herself busy. After settling back into her nest, she began basic renovations, fetching new nesting material, scraping out the old lining to make space for fresh bedding, especially the nest bowl in the middle. She hunted, too, for brown trout or pike, feeding well and often, as she needed to do to build up her strength after her migration and prepare her for the rigours of the breeding season ahead. The day after she arrived, however, she had a fight with a buzzard that had strayed too close to the nest. A dramatic and brief aerial dogfight ensued, and the intruder was dispatched in no uncertain terms.

Before her arrival, ospreys had been spotted: one female had even landed on the nest, then flown off. One persistent female intruder, however, began to take liberties, landing regularly on it. Lady appeared to allow her the freedom to come and go – or, rather, she tolerated her. She was clearly not happy with the new development, evident in all the defensive behaviour she displayed – mantling, or drooping, her wings, and posturing by standing very erect, extended neck, raised back feathers, partially open wings beating slowly – it led to an occasional chase, to the accompaniment of her alarm-calling. Occasional high drama at Osprey Towers that spring was acceptable, but this time it begged a question: was this new female a serious rival for the nest?

Time alone would tell. For now Lady managed to keep her nest without her mate to back her up. But although she would see off the young female every now and then, it seemed sometimes that her heart was not really in it; as if she somehow accepted the other bird's presence in her nest and, indeed, almost welcomed it. Perhaps she knew at an intuitive level that she needed to secure her succession. In any case, the female intruder returned continuously for several weeks; her regular appearances seemed to confirm she was in the area looking for a nest of her own. She was a beautiful bird – huge, with very dark markings and a distinctive black cap, possibly one of Lady's chicks from a previous year, although, generally, female birds go further afield than their original homes or nest sites. Sometimes, though, they return to the nest – as Lady herself might have done two decades earlier. If so, the intruder had arrived too soon. Two's company; three's a crowd.

Events at Osprey Towers prompted chat and comment on the Lowes osprey blog especially, but amid the chatter something was not aired, something so patently obvious that no one had the heart to voice it – just in case, somehow, that made it come true: what if Lady did not make it back one year? The new female osprey was quite a beauty, and not even Lady, so beloved, so tenacious, so fierce, so tender, so connected to life and determined to live it to the full, could go on for ever. Any such notions were soon swept aside, but re-emerged as the season passed, casting a long shadow over Lowes that year.

That spring, however, there was nothing about Lady, apart from her advanced years, that gave much sense of her mortality. She had come back to Lowes in fighting form, intent on defending a nest that had been hers for nearly two decades. It was a war she had to win and was conducted mostly in the air, a fierce, locked-talon struggle in which she and her rivals tumbled down and down into freefall, before, at the very last moment, letting go. Those battles were thrilling to watch – nerve-racking, too – but no one believed

Lady would ever lose them. She seemed invincible, partly because she had secured that nest for so long, which made her the dominant female in that corner of Perthshire.

Although Lady was often the first back, when her migration was slow she had to face the consequences. One year Eric had returned first and mated with a new, red-ringed female bird. A few days later an unringed female flew in: Lady. She swiftly kicked the new girl out and resumed her partnership with Eric as if nothing had happened. Each year's breeding season produced its own little twist, and the following year there was a twist on the twist, bringing a touch of TV soap to Lowes: Lady returned from migration with a yellow-ringed male in tow and proceeded to mate with him. What's sauce for the gander is sauce for the goose. Revenge was sweet – all the sweeter because that year, 2008, Lowes had a new high-definition screen on which to view it all.

But although the HD stayed, the new male did not. The following morning Eric returned. The yellow-ringed rival was sent packing, then Lady and Eric began home improvements on a nest damaged by the preceding stormy winter. Such seasonal ups and downs were part of the rich tapestry of life on the nest, and Lady and Eric had survived a number throughout their years together. But nothing lasts for ever. As spring 2010 continued, it became clear that Eric would never return; that Lady had won her fight for the nest against a bigger, stronger, younger female that, one day, might depose her. But that day had not come.

Lady would have put all thought of Eric behind her when her instinct reminded her that her biological clock was ticking. She would have known that time was running out and that she needed to accept a new mate or risk not breeding that year. The sooner the breeding cycle began, the better chance of a happy outcome. Lady's breeding record was good, and her partnership with Eric had worked, so she hung on for him. The first week passed and she had chased off a string of suitors. If she did not find a mate soon, it would be difficult to continue to defend the nest, especially with that warning shot across her bows from the young female who was so willing to step into her shoes.

On 4 April a new boy arrived on the block. His ID ring established that he was local, from Ballinluig, some seven miles north-west of Lowes, near Pitlochry. He had been ringed (dark green with white 7Y on the left leg) on behalf of Tay Ringing Group conservation charity by Keith Brockie, a local wildlife artist and illustrator and dedicated field naturalist who, since the late 1980s, had monitored and ringed ospreys and done a lot else to assist their successful repopulation. On 16 July 2000 he had ringed this bird with number 1337908, one of a brood of three chicks. Brockie posted a blog on the Lowes online osprey diary in April 2010, saying that such sightings show the value of colour-ringing individual birds because they can be traced over their lifespan. Coincidentally, he had built the base of the Lowes nest that the new male bird was about to try and occupy.

The male osprey had fledged ten years earlier but no sightings of him had been recorded anywhere since his ring date in either West Africa, Perthshire or the Highlands, until his appearance in Lowes. Although most juvenile ospreys, fledged in Scotland, spend the first three years of their lives in West Africa after their initial migration, Roy Dennis, in *A Life of Ospreys*, records sightings one year in England of two one-year-olds. Most two-year-olds probably do return to the UK and Europe throughout spring and summer and some will wander into northern nesting grounds to sniff them out but they do not stay to breed.

After his years in the south, Lady's new suitor had perhaps returned to Perthshire a few times – migrant site fidelity is profound – and might have bred nearby; perhaps his usual female had not returned that year. Alternatively, he might have been ready to breed for the first time in his third year, but the shortage of natural nests might have prevented it. At his age, ten, he should have been successful, because he was a mature bird, but he seemed inexperienced and unaware of his role. If Lady were to take him on, it would be up to her, an alpha female, to train him to perfection – or somewhere near it. He could not have had a better teacher – but was he the best bet for the elderly Lady?

The new male's propositioning was not greeted with wholehearted joy by Lady's fans, who, the osprey team and bloggers at least, still hankered after the tried-and-tested Eric. Lady and Eric had fitted together like a comfy pair of slippers, a proven partnership that knew how to navigate each other's strengths and weaknesses. The prospect of life, especially new life, without Eric pointed to an uncertain future. Would this prove to be the end of Lady's long run of breeding success at Lowes? With any other bird, it might have done, but Lady was no quitter. Her instinct to breed was much greater than her loyalty to her mate. After a week or so, pragmatically, she took on her new male partner, accepting his presence on the nest, and opted to throw in her lot with him. As did the Lowes osprey bloggers, who christened him Laird. And so, with barely a backward glance, Lady and Laird's courtship began.

Ospreys breed more successfully when they have somewhere they can call home. Some young adult ospreys do not breed even when they are capable of doing so – Laird's probable fate – preferring to delay until they find somewhere they like, perhaps having to wait for an established nest, as Laird had done. Ospreys are generally sociable and like to nest near to each other; if necessary, however, they can cope as solitary nesters. In ornithological terms, this makes them semi-colonial. If given a choice, young adult ospreys favour an established nest in a colony, or build a nest nearby, partly because of the area's proven suitability. They also prefer an older, experienced mate, much like Lady, although rarely quite as old: ospreys usually do not live so long. Studies, especially of the more established osprey colonies in Scotland, give an average age of first breeding at about four years old for the female (four and a half for males). North American studies bear this out, with first breeding around the age of four or five. For Lady, it was a good thing that osprey males appreciated the virtues of an older mate and that she had been able to recognize a good nest when she first saw one and had stuck with it.

Once ospreys settle at a nest site, the heart of their courtship – mating and feeding – begins. Mating occurs any time, anywhere, and often on the nest, because that is where the female bird spends much of her time. If the sky dance is foreplay fireworks, the sex itself is fast and furious, lasting just a few seconds. There may be calling, from one or both birds – perhaps the male is solicited by the female bird, which crouches low, shivering her wings, tipping forwards a little and raising her tail. The male, talons drawn considerately in, lands, hopefully gently, lightly, on her back. Until the date of the first egg laid, the birds may mate frequently, many, many times, with things hotting up just prior to egg-laying, then slowing down on the day of laying and continuing until the last egg has been laid.

Lady and Laird mated constantly for ten days – the usual time between first mating and first egg. Laird seemed to know what he was doing, but it became clear that he was not so accomplished when it came to other aspects of the partnership: he was hopeless at catching fish. The fairly clear division of labour during the breeding season usually means that the male osprey provides the food for the female as she sits on the nest, brings material to build or maintain the nest, and helps protect it from intruders. The male birds deliver fish to the nest initially to impress their female partners, as part of their courtship ritual, to prove that they can keep the larder stocked. Courtship feeding's main purpose, apparently, is to ensure mate fidelity and encourage the female to stay on the nest; it may also mean healthier eggs. In any case, hunting should be second nature to the male because a plentiful supply of fish is vital for the birds after their long migration and before the demands of the breeding season, for which both birds must be in good condition.

Since Laird's arrival, the Lowes osprey team had been watching, with some apprehension, Lady train her inexperienced mate. She had her work cut out and her repeated calls of displeasure – *quee-quee-quee* – encouraged him to work harder and make that year's nest a productive one. Lady had accepted a young upstart, and now everyone hoped that she knew what she was doing.

An osprey hunting for fish is a phenomenal sight. In his classic work, *Wild Sports and Natural History of the Highlands* (1845), Charles St John describes how 'this very beautiful bird drops like a stone on any unlucky fish that its sharp eye may detect in the clear pools of the river, and I believe she seldom pounces in vain.' It is magical – spellbinding – to watch an osprey plunge into a lake or river, feet or, sometimes, head first at more than forty miles per hour and emerge carrying a fish in a sparkling spray of water. The sheer grace and impressive technical expertise add to the mystique. The osprey's angled wings and long wing feathers are designed for the dive jolt and effort of yanking a live fish from the water. Ospreys are seriously strong birds: their long, high-arching wings and muscular greenish-grey legs give them the power to transport fish as heavy as they are, although their usual prey is around 15–30 per cent of their bodyweight. Their razor-sharp black talons, which snap shut in a fraction of a second, enable them to hold on to it. Anyone who has ever had the pleasure of holding a young osprey can feel the muscles in its legs even at six weeks old. (According to Roy Dennis, they will also notice that the females are calmer and more trusting, particularly when hooded, though ever observant if not, while the males are more volatile – they struggle and complain, even if hooded.)

The long, unfeathered tarsi (part of the leg) enable the bird to reach deep into the water at the end of its plunge. The osprey has joints in its feet that facilitate the manoeuvre and grip of its two flexible, reversible outer toes on a slippery, struggling live fish, with two toes forward and two back. The distinctively scaly or prickly skin of the foot pad and toes provides a Velcro-like spiny grip.

The strong, compact black bill, sharply hooked for tearing fish apart and twisting off bite-size pieces, looks and is scary – even a chick has a sharp beak. But the feet, big and strong, the four toes equipped with large, well-curved talons, are more dangerous. They are the osprey's hunting weapons, allied, of course, to the bird's extraordinary eyesight, with its clarity and depth perception, which it can use with pinpoint accuracy to dive from a hundred feet, able to see from there into the shallows to grab a slithering fish and lift it nimbly from the water.

Most ospreys choose to hunt actively on the wing, which is usually more fruitful than perching and waiting for fish to heave into view. Depending on which fish they are trying to catch, they hunt from between fifteen and 150 feet above the water, catching their prey from a range of freshwater and marine species that includes perch, pike, trout, carp or roach and, in coastal estuaries, flatfish, such as flounder, and pollack. They also hunt mullet. Indeed the osprey was once called the mullet hawk in southern England, and it is mullet that makes up a large part of its diet during its winters in Africa. Ospreys are opportunistic in their choice of prey. On Tiran Island, effectively a nature reserve on the Red Sea at the southern tip of the Gulf of Aqaba, they have expanded their menu to include massive spider conch, which, in a tactic observed among crows and gulls, they open by dropping them from heights of more than a hundred feet on to hard surfaces such as cement-filled oil drums.

The size of their catch varies, sometimes as heavy as two pounds (about half their bodyweight), but more commonly four to eight ounces. The birds are able to dive to a maximum of three feet deep so they hunt fish that school near the surface or inhabit shallow waters. Their fishing style, which immerses them in water, may even submerge them fully, making them unique among birds of prey. They are adapted for it: their underside feathers are especially close set, oily and dense to keep them dry and prevent waterlogging, although even this is no defence against perpetual plunging dives or driving rain.

With their prey secured, the birds emerge from their dive and briefly shake off the water in mid-flight. They fly with their catch ensnared in their fearsome feet, one of which they hold in front of the other. Their prey, which is still alive and struggling for life, is carried head facing forward, body tucked close, to minimize air resistance and maximize speed on the way back to the perch or nest.

It has been said that to see an osprey catching a fish is to see God. But Laird had issues about fishing. In fairness, it was still cold that early April: the loch had thawed only a few days before Lady had come back in late March, and it took a good month for the water to warm to a reasonable temperature. The fish were very low below the surface, and the ones Laird caught initially were small. Lady was more capable than Laird at catching big fish, and people were puzzled as to why she had decided to accept him as her mate: had her instincts let her down?

Over the years, Lady's mates would have hunted fish for both of them. The male generally takes the catch back to a preferred perching post in the nest area, then starts to feed himself, holding the fish down against the post, twisting and pulling at it, ripping off small pieces of flesh with his hooked bill. He feeds for about half an hour, always starting with the head, and eats about half of the fish. Then he delivers the rest to the nest, after which the female leaves for a chosen perch to finish it, discarding the guts and any particularly big bones; the smaller ones are edible as the osprey has a tough digestive tract. After feeding she will clean her bill and feet, and do a bit of feather preening; sometimes, in flight afterwards, she will dip into the water to rinse off any fishy bits stuck between her toes.

It was a good life, especially at Lowes with its abundant source of pike and brown trout – or the increasingly available rainbow trout from nearby fish farms. Laird's arrival had not produced any sky-dance spectacular, as there was no nest to secure and Lady was already upon it, but the other element of courtship, hunting, was not about a slick performance: it was about survival. If Laird could not become more proficient at providing for Lady, there would be trouble.

5 A new season

A fine matriarch like Lady deserved a fine mate. That was the view on the Lowes osprey blog, and Lady was trying to train her new young partner to be just that. When, early on, he started bringing in the odd stick for nest repair, this was a good sign that the pair bond between them was strengthening, even though fish deliveries were random. But the less capable Laird seemed of bringing in big fish to impress Lady, the more big sticks he fetched. That year's nest was a wonder.

After throwing in her lot with Laird that first week in April, Lady had spent more time in the nest, regally ensconced on her throne of thick twigs, leaving it for just the odd, quick stretch, settling into domestic mode prior, it was hoped, to egg-laying. After a slow start, Laird was making several flights a day for new material. In manipulating one especially long and unwieldy twig, he accidentally hit Lady and had to escape at record speed as she loudly voiced her displeasure. The nest was becoming a spacious sprawl, as cavernous as anyone could remember it, and extremely narrow. Laird seemed intent on burying Lady, smothering her in his enthusiasm for his building project and for keeping her safe – perverse confirmation of Oscar Wilde's belief that we always kill the thing we love.

The nest would flatten out once the chicks arrived; it was normal for it to be high-sided early in the breeding season. Osprey nests have to be robust, because they are built in exposed sites, in trees and atop existing man-made structures, such as electricity pylons, transmission masts and stone towers, so their stability depends on their substantial size and weight. In Scotland, most of the tree-top nests start out about a foot high and three feet wide; they grow ever taller with the annual home improvements, which makes them especially vulnerable to wind and weather. Cliff-tops and crags (on which ospreys have never so far nested in Britain), ground and man-made nests, like Lady's, can be even bigger, up to six feet wide and three high. The birds sometimes ground-nest on small islands or other places with no ground predators; indeed, globally, a substantial number of ospreys are island nesters: there, they tend to build nests near to one another either in trees, low down, or sometimes on the ground.

Some osprey nests last for decades; those on rocky summits and remote islands for much longer – centuries, even. They weigh, surprisingly, an average four hundred pounds, sometimes as much as six hundred – perhaps ospreys build not for a season but for posterity.

Given the dimensions of the Lowes nest, there was no chance of Lady falling out of it, as had happened the previous spring to a female goshawk in an English forest, blown out by high winds as she brooded her chicks. As the nest was located a vulnerable fifty feet up a tree, it was probably not without precedent, but there was a happy ending: feathers ruffled, she returned, unharmed, to her chicks. This was not a scenario that would play out this year at Lowes, if Laird had any say in it.

If Laird was obsessed with nest building, he was not alone. At the end of the second week in April, a blue tit at Lowes was also seen hard at work building its nest, turning it into something quite luxurious. Blue tits like to nest in small holes or narrow cracks in trees, and, more quirkily, in drainpipes and letterboxes. On this occasion the site was a nest box.

Birds were busy everywhere. On the osprey blog, one correspondent, from distant Vancouver, who had visited Dunkeld and Lowes every November for ten years, wrote about the birds in her backyard, a family of scrub jays that raised chicks each year, the hummingbirds she had year-round, the mourning doves, the numerous bright yellow goldfinches and rosy-red purple finches (once described as a 'sparrow dipped in raspberry juice' by one of the world's pre-eminent naturalists, North American ornithologist Roger Tory Peterson). There was a lot to see at Lowes too:

it was easy to glimpse great spotted woodpeckers, pheasants and red squirrels from the visitor centre.

A rumour was circulating that during the previous winter a white-tailed eagle, a red-list rare breeding bird, had landed briefly on Lady's nest. There are many similarities between this eagle and the osprey, often confused in traditional stories as both were sometimes classified as 'eagle fishers'. In Scotland, the white-tailed eagle, also known as the sea eagle, prefers to nest in trees; it had also been declared extinct in the UK during the early nineteenth century, due to illegal killing and persecution by gamekeepers, shepherds, fisheries, egg and skin collectors. Once widespread, in the UK the last breeding white-tailed eagle had been recorded in Scotland in 1916 – as, of course, had the osprey. It, too, was receiving help to return, specifically via a reintroduction programme that had started in 1975; in the decade that followed, eighty-two young white-tailed eagles, from Norway, were released on the Isle of Rum in the Inner Hebrides, with the first successful breeding in 1985. Since then several pairs had nested successfully each year. Further releases in the 1990s in Wester Ross in the north-west Highlands ensured that the population would become self-sustaining. The birds had been limited to Scotland's west coast, although a reintroduction programme had started in east Scotland (from where the interloper on Lady's nest might have come). These eagles are so rare – a recorded fifty territorial pairs, only in Scotland, by 2010 – that even a single nest loss is a significant setback.

Like the osprey, the white-tailed eagle is a big bird, although the eagle is by far the bigger of the two, about three feet long to the osprey's two, and celebrated as the UK's largest bird of prey with an amazing eight-foot wingspan (to the osprey's five-foot and the wandering albatross's record eleven-plus) – it has been described as a barn door in flight. Both birds need and build large nests of a similar size.

When Peter Ferns visited Lady's nest at close quarters one day, climbing to the top of the tree to remove the chicks for ringing, he was comfortably able to lie down in it, to the possible surprise of the three chicks in residence. Over the years its size has changed continually, as use, time and winter weather have taken their toll. Nest conditions at the start of each new breeding season depend on what winter has done to it during the osprey's absence. Sometimes the birds return in spring to find they have lost none of their home – if that happens, the nests can grow vast.

It is the female who wedges and weaves the fresh nesting material into place; the male does the fetching and carrying. The birds use virtually whatever they find, foraging for branches or sticks, twigs, grass, moss and bark, fishing net, tyre, rope, string and plastic. The bigger branches and thicker sticks provide the structure; moss, leaves, straw, rushes, pondweed and similar softer items are used to line the inner cup. Although the birds share nest-building, the male bird is generally busier earlier in the season and later on becomes preoccupied with fishing, while the female does most running repairs. It is a job that is key to the birds' survival and reproduction. Even when clutches fail, the adults can be seen devotedly nest-gathering and mending, or building a new nest or 'frustration eyrie', forward planning for better luck in the next breeding season.

An osprey nest stands out a mile. The enormous lattice tangle at Lowes is no exception, which, at sixty-foot high, is not overly lofty. Whatever the height, the birds like a 360-degree view. They are quite paranoid – with good reason – about security, but as long as they can see everything around them, they are content. Scotland's most celebrated and beautiful eyrie location is the romantic ruins of an old castle on the island at Loch an Eilein in the forest of Rothiemurchus, Speyside (where, after ruthless persecution, ospreys nest again). As tree-dwellers, it is vital that the birds have a forest habitat in which to nest as well as water in which to hunt. One failing of Scottish forests – or, rather, of modern forestry practice – is that the trees are all uniformly conical and do not have the broad, domed crown and lovely big lateral branches of Scotland's native Scots pines that make ideal osprey nesting platforms.

There is a limited supply of the right trees and nest sites in Scotland as the country has been so heavily deforested, especially in comparison with areas of Scandinavia, which has extensive pine forests and countless lakes. Sweden, for instance, has a relative abundance of suitable nest sites and, not surprisingly, is home to Europe's largest osprey population, with an estimated 3,300–3,600 breeding pairs –

although in the 1960s the birds did suffer losses owing to the effects of pesticide use.

Although ospreys nest in other conifers, they favour the tall and slender Scots pine, especially the flat tops of tall, dead trees, because the open space above their nest gives them room to manoeuvre. Ospreys' long, narrow wings are not designed for landing or taking off in tight spaces. The Scots pine's broad, wide top becomes squashed as the tree ages and offers a strong and secure base on which to build a nest and take off from it.

Indeed it is generally a valued tree, for people and wildlife. It was once much in demand for shipbuilding, and its resin was also used to make pitch for sealing beer casks. It is an excellent habitat for stump lichen and insects, such as narrow-headed ants and Scottish wood ants, that grow around and live in the cracks on the trunk; birds such as the siskin, great spotted woodpecker, crested tit and crossbill can feed well from it, as can, specifically in Scotland, the wryneck and capercaillie that are to be found in some pinewoods. As an evergreen tree, the pine has been seen as a symbol of immortality; indeed, the high resin content of its sap means that the wood is slow to decay. Perhaps the osprey were on to something when they picked this species for their nests.

Ospreys are clearly capable of selecting their own trees and building their own nests, but they have also been assisted in this by conservationists, better to enable them to recolonize more of their former historic range and help the species recover. Initially, conservation nest work was all about making repairs – for example, when the Lowes nest first fell foul of that May weather back in 1970 – but nests are often now built from scratch (following conservation rules and requiring a special conservation licence to visit after completion, if they are tenanted, or even subsequently to repair the nest).

Through work done in the Highlands, osprey conservationists have realized that artificial nesting platforms, effectively starter-kit homes, in trees or elsewhere, will help ospreys to get a foothold in new places. Ospreys quite readily tenant them; many are in regular use in Scotland and elsewhere, partly because of the limited availability of suitable trees. In fact, nest platforms have become a key element of ongoing conservation work with ospreys, a big help to the birds while they are still relatively rare breeders. They are built to appeal to migrating birds as they fly over; the hope is to attract them in.

During autumn and winter conservation groups, rangers and enthusiasts all over the UK as well as in Europe and the US look to erect more platforms to attract more young ospreys to take up residence in new areas. These include wooden bases, big enough to hold a nest, often covered by a cocoon of wire mesh for extra strength. Sometimes branches, twigs and moss are interwoven to recreate a genuine osprey nest and make it easy for the birds. In some places, including Scotland, but especially North America, Germany and Australia, where the birds like to nest on electricity pylons, there are specially designed metal baskets fit for purpose, which can be bolted atop a pylon or pole, ready for the birds to build in them. Ospreys also like a duty perch: a protruding branch or pole from the nest or nearby, an osprey version of a ship's mast crow's nest lookout platform, from which they can keep a vigilant eye on what's happening around them. Man-made nest sites can be put in obvious but still remote locations, where the birds have the best chance of success without too much disturbance. Given human responsibility for eliminating them from the UK – and other places around the world where they used to thrive – the osprey deserve a helping hand.

Someone who has done more than most to encourage them back to their ancestral ranges is Roy Dennis. For his services to conservation, he was awarded the RSPB's prestigious Golden Eagle award and made an MBE in 2004. He formed the Highland Foundation for Wildlife in 1995 as a charitable trust dedicated to wildlife conservation and research, with a special emphasis on species-recovery projects and the restoration of natural ecosystems. It was in 1960 that he built his first artificial nest, in Scotland, at Loch Garten, from an old cartwheel, an early prototype for the subsequent nesting platforms. No bird would go near it, perhaps because, as he admits, he neglected to soften the cup with the grass, moss, leaf litter and rotted straw that make a nest a home. He learnt from his mistake and has built – and repaired – a huge number since.

At the moment the big growth areas for the UK's osprey population are not the Highlands, where they have been settled for a while now, but southern Scotland, the Borders, Dumfries and Galloway. The breeding grounds are centred on Scotland, but there is a move to increase the birds' spread to other parts of the UK, including the Lake District, and beyond. Conservationists in southern England are experimenting with innovative polystyrene models of ospreys as decoys to tempt in live birds. In Dorset, five six-foot-wide stick nests were built at the top of forty-foot trees in Arne RSPB reserve, near Poole Harbour (with an extra two for good measure at the harbour itself). Two life-size poly-ospreys were added to the show-home nests, which were also customized with white paint to give them the lived-in guano look that is so attractive to the birds. The Dorset coast was selected because it is on the migration route, back and forth, to osprey wintering grounds south of the Sahara, and the birds are often seen there at migration time, perching on posts and in trees. It also has the necessary copious fish supply.

The Arne trials are an exciting development, with which Roy Dennis has been closely involved. The scheme has worked at other locations in Europe. Perhaps the osprey will re-inhabit England's south coast one day, but this is a long-term project, and no one will know for several years whether or not it is destined for success. Many fake nests may never be used – but if at first they don't succeed, then it's a case of try, try, try again. If the Arne experiment works, it will be beneficial to the bird's population and range in the UK, giving it a foothold on Britain's most southerly edge, a perfect geographical counterpoint to their northerly Scottish strongholds.

The Arne approach to osprey conservation works best if the artificial nests are located near to where ospreys are known to pass in spring and autumn, in the right place with the right habitat. A key area on the osprey migration route is the Scottish Borders, where Lowes' seasonal ranger Emma Rawling became involved in an osprey conservation project. A few years ago there was not a single pair in the area, but birds would always stop off on the River Tweed as a rest stage on their migratory route. Artificial nesting platforms attracted them to the area, and by 2009 there were twelve breeding pairs. There have been other similar success stories across the UK, in the Lake District, Northumbria and Rutland, thanks to the work of dedicated teams of conservationists, like Rawling and Dennis.

Quite sensibly, ospreys would rather choose a ready-made nest than start from scratch. Studies have shown that inexperienced adults are more likely to occupy a fake nest, then advertise for a mate, than to start a new colony all on their own. The birds typically spread at a slow rate, as they prefer to join existing colonies by replacing birds that die or fail to return from migration. In his work for his Highland Foundation for Wildlife, from his base near the River Findhorn, Roy Dennis travels abroad frequently to advise on conservation projects. He and his foundation helped with reintroductions to Spain and advised on projects in Italy and Portugal.

When asked about his osprey translocation work in 2004, he described how, in certain places in Scotland, such as Strathspey, young ospreys, liking to return to breed where they fledged, come back to their old homes and end up competing for nests and nest sites. Fights break out, in which eggs and nests are damaged; sometimes the battles are so fierce that a bird dies in its attempt to gain control of a nest. In an echo of what may have happened to Laird, some birds were not managing to breed until they were at least seven.

To Roy Dennis, redistribution by translocation, involving the transfer of young ospreys shortly before they fledge to a new site suitable for breeding, was sensible wildlife management. In Europe, translocation was pioneered in England at Rutland Water from 1996. Successful reintroductions in North America also provided a blueprint, and there are ongoing projects now in several countries.

Ospreys had suffered population decline throughout North America and Europe, and reached their lowest ebb in the mid-1950s. During the first part of the twentieth century they had been persecuted to extinction in much of southern Europe. Following numerous conservation projects, their population is now increasing in most of Europe, but they are still rare in the south, which is ripe for further reintroductions – indeed, they have been taking place. In Germany, ospreys are on the German red list of breeding birds, as a species of conservation concern. In the 1970s there were only around seventy pairs. However, following conservation projects in all German states, this number had risen to around 550 by 2010 and is increasing rapidly.

In Spain, there had been no ospreys nesting on the mainland since the 1950s, although the birds had never become extinct in the Balearic or Canary Islands. There, in 2009, they were clinging on with twenty and twelve pairs respectively. By 1999 on the Iberian peninsula, however, there was just one nesting pair, in Portugal. The five osprey chicks that were flown from Scotland to Spain in 2006 were part of a plan to put things right.

The young birds' journey was one more step in an important restoration project for southern European osprey, which had started in 2003 as an initiative of the Andalucían government, between the Doñana Biological Station in southern Spain and Roy Dennis's Highland Foundation for Wildlife. The birds had been collected from nest sites in Scotland and were flown out from Inverness, via Gatwick airport, to Málaga, and taken to a release site at a water reservoir near Cádiz, where they were joined by other young ospreys from Finland and Germany until they were ready for release. By spending the few crucial weeks post-fledging there, the young birds would consider the new site their home, the place to which they would return eighteen months or more later. A similar project had begun that summer in Italy, where French and Italian ornithologists translocated young ospreys from Corsica to La

Maremma National Park in Tuscany. Dennis's Highland Foundation for Wildlife assisted with the planning and development of this project too.

The translocations to Spain eventually turned up trumps. In June 2009 ospreys bred in mainland Spain for the first time in eighty years when three chicks were born in the Marismas del Odiel, in Huelva, and two in Cádiz. Since 2003, more than a hundred chicks had been released in Cádiz and Huelva from Germany, Finland and Scotland. The young ospreys released in Andalucía, its huge reservoirs providing a suitable habitat for them, had shown the normal migratory behaviour of birds raised in their own nests in the region and had started to fly south to known osprey areas. Radio-tracking located them on the West African coast along rivers in Senegal and Gambia.

France, too, once had a big osprey population. By the first half of the twentieth century they were a rare sight, not seen as a nesting bird on the French mainland after the Second World War. But in summer 1984, Swedish raptor devotee Rolf Wahl, then living in France, discovered a pair of ospreys building a nest at L'Étang du Ravoir in the former royal hunting forest of Orléans, near Ouzouer-sur-Loire. It was perfect osprey breeding ground, with its abundant mature pine trees and hunting in lakes along the River Loire. Appreciating the significance of his find, Wahl fought for and won protection as well as monitoring for the nest site with the result that the pair, thought to have originated in Germany, bred successfully the following year; other pairs subsequently joined the fledgling colony. So committed was he to the cause that Wahl moved to the area, giving up his business in Paris to work with the osprey in the Loire valley, where he has remained ever since.

In the mid-1990s, a second colony started in a forest around Château de Chambord, down the Loire to the west, past Orléans. Then two more nests appeared on electricity pylons outside the forests, and one in Essonne in the Île-de-France region towards Paris. In 2009 there was another new nest in Moselle, near the German border, making an official French mainland total of twenty-five that year – and, hopefully, rising; some suspect there are nests on private properties too but, if so, they are secret. The Orléans ospreys had been helped by, among other things, the construction of artificial nests. In fact, by 2010, most of the nests there were man-made.

The Scottish Wildlife Trust, to which the Lowes reserve belongs, did its own bit of nest building and expanding when it developed the small loch at the northern edge of the valley of Strathmore, its shoreline and surrounding wood-land, as one of its first nature reserves. It is no surprise that Lady thrived there. It is osprey heaven, a des-res for a bird that asks no more than somewhere to nest undisturbed and to fish with ease.

In front of the visitor centre, which sits just behind the observation hides that edge the loch, there is an untidy, in-your-face pile of sticks about six feet in diameter: a huge interwoven sprawl of twigs and small branches, with a deep, soft inlay of moss, bark, dry grass and pond weed at its centre. This is a ground-level mock-up of Lady's nest, usually only visible from afar, atop a tall tree, and it is impressively huge – indeed, the size of a double bed. In the visitor centre, a large closed-circuit TV screen makes it easy to view close-ups of osprey family life on the nest, in the surrounding trees and along the waters of the loch.

Throughout the breeding season the eyrie is visible, via a non-invasive nest camera, on screens in the visitor centre and on the Trust's website. Thousands of people come to Lowes each breeding season to enjoy the osprey and other wildlife in a natural setting and, crucially, in an environment that is safe and offers minimal disturbance for nesting birds. Each new season brings fresh experiences and its own specific jobs, even after the osprey migrate towards summer's end.

One such task was checking the robustness of Lady's nest, the metal base of which had been constructed by Keith Brockie, who had colour-ringed Laird in 2000. Brockie had built the nest base, in 1989–90, ensuring that it was strong enough to survive the winter storms and the weight of the snow. He had made its outer casing from the wires of an old tattie, or potato, basket, weaving through the unravelled canes of the basket and a few intertwined wooden sticks, then adding the obligatory splash of guano-white paint. The nest, on its secure and stable base, had stood the test of time and worked as an osprey magnet; by 2010 it was still in place on the tree, unlike the nest it had replaced, which had been damaged beyond repair.

Lady had been breeding in Brockie's nest longer and more productively than any other female osprey on a UK site, so it was regarded as an unqualified success. By the end of 2010's breeding season, however, there was evident strain on the containing branch as the nest had become hugely heavy, hardly surprising given Laird's zealous stick fetching. There was not an ounce of give in Lady's nest any more; Peter Ferns had stood on it – as he sometimes did, to test its strength and resilience – and, while a normal branch would show some resilience, the nest branch did not budge. It was not dead, but it was bearing as much weight as it would take and at serious risk of snapping. There was a plan afoot to shore it up.

It was likely, perhaps, that Keith Brockie might strengthen what he had first assembled two decades earlier. His nest had certainly stood the test of time, as had his enthusiasm for wildlife, not just ringing the birds and making their nests but painting and drawing them too. As an acclaimed wildlife artist and illustrator, he liked to work without disturbing the birds, observing them in their own space and therefore able to portray them as they were.

For Brockie, the challenge of working with unpredictable wildlife was integral to the overall delight of being part of the natural world. As a naturalist and artist, he has spent most of his life in the great outdoors, equally at ease drawing and painting birds as climbing high to reach a nest and ring the legs of their young or even build their nests for them. The nest he had made at Lowes had attracted Lady and her mate in spring 1991; now, almost twenty years later, in the spring of 2010, she was about to lay a brand-new clutch of eggs in it.

6 Fifty and counting

Lady had always been one to exceed expectations; now she had done so again. It was on an unlucky-for-some 13 April that Lowes' osprey HQ announced that their female bird had settled into the nest that morning and looked suspiciously as if she was ready to lay an egg. The thirteenth had been a lucky laying day for Lady before. Three years earlier, on Friday, 13 April 2007, to the great delight of the Lowes team, she had laid the first egg of that breeding season. Her success now was all the more welcome: expectations had been growing that her laying days were over. Not only had she laid an unexpected egg but also broken yet another record.

Lady had spent much of the preceding weekend preparing the nest for laying – making the central cup ever deeper by scraping it out with her feet and endlessly rearranging sticks and twigs around the edge. She had spent a great deal of the Monday fixing the soft grass and moss lining to the bowl, and finally settled into it early on Tuesday morning. This was all normal behaviour prior to laying; its imminence was further confirmed by the timing. Ospreys in Britain tend to lay their eggs between mid-April and early May – further north, in Finland, for instance, they lay a bit later; the further south they breed, the earlier they lay.

Laying an egg is rarely either quick or easy, but that was what Lady did, with apparent speed and ease, early on the Tuesday morning. It was a whole ten minutes before she revealed her brand-new egg to the world via the webcam. Even without the close-up view afforded by nest cameras, it was always possible to know when the eggs first arrived, because incubating birds stand around less on the nest edge than they do when courting, instead sinking deep into the nest bowl to keep the eggs warm.

Laird soon dropped in for a paternal visit. He had taken to perching on a pine tree a few hundred yards away, which he used as a lookout and regular resting post; he was often there during the day, when he was not away fishing, perching, osprey-style, on one leg with the other pulled up and tucked within his feathers. Ospreys like to perch. Perhaps it restores them for the rigours of flight, which takes ten times more energy than an equivalent time spent perching. Then there was the demand on their energy resources from hunting, which is labour- and time-intensive. It would be Laird's job from now on to bring in regular food supplies. When he delivered Lady's share of the fish, she would perch outside the nest to feed. With the arrival of the first egg, she had to keep the nest clean and fresh to avoid attracting scavengers.

Such was the joy at Lady's success, so special and legendary a bird was she, that one of her blogger fans suggested she deserved a bronze statue in pride of place at Lowes' visitor centre. But there would be no memorials just yet: there was too much life in the old girl (as the BBC news acknowledged that day, referring to her as 'the UK's oldest-known breeding female osprey'). She was a truly individual bird, a wonder of nature. Her fifty-sixth egg, in her mid-twenties, had surprised national wildlife experts, not least those at Lowes, who had doubted her fertility, given that most ospreys produce about twenty eggs over a lifetime. Lady was doing her best to repopulate her species.

The next two days turned into an emotional rollercoaster ride, as initial elation morphed into concern about Laird's commitment and skills as a father. At first he delivered the same fish many times, trying to interest Lady in food, but she was reluctant to take it, apparently not wanting to leave her precious egg. She left him in charge only when she was really hungry. It was a trying time, but she was so diligent a parent that some of that would surely rub off on Laird. It was possible, after all, that he just needed practice and encouragement, given that this might be his first-ever egg.

From laying to hatching would take five to six weeks; incubation is shared, and the female birds invariably do nights, the males taking over for some of the daylight hours. The male bird's stint on the eggs lets the female leave the nest to feed and exercise. Ospreys do not risk leaving their eggs uncovered for long, perhaps because their nests are so open and exposed to predators and the elements.

Initially, Laird did not have a clue when it came to taking his turn at guarding the eggs and keeping them warm; Lowes blog posters nicknamed him Clueless. Lady would take any fish he delivered to feed elsewhere but he would often stand in the nest and walk about. Left alone with the first egg, he seemed reluctant to sit on it, taking an eternity to settle, eventually, tenderly, tucking the egg beneath his feathers and positioning his talons so as not to harm it. When he did settle down, he did so with great care.

There were spells, however, when he would fly off and leave the eggs unattended, but Lady's breeding experience stood her in good stead, and she was never too far away, heading back to the nest if she sensed danger, flying in and making a racket, as if she were scolding Laird for his sloppy ways. It was not a workable arrangement, and the pair had to come to a better understanding if damage to egg or nest was to be avoided.

By the early hours of 16 April, there was another egg. Before its appearance Lady had been preparing herself: shuffling, panting, straining, wings oddly angled, peeping and making low noises, then hunkering down. She looked majestic now atop her two eggs. With Lady's age and Laird's inexperience, perhaps two would suffice this time –

but she was likely to lay three. At first breeding, in their initial clutch, young female ospreys usually produce two eggs; in subsequent years, when they are more mature, they lay three.

Osprey clutch sizes vary from three eggs, most often, to two, sometimes, and four, infrequently, for which the female bird must be in prime condition. Interestingly, smaller birds of prey lay a greater number of eggs in each clutch: the UK's smallest raptor, the merlin – like the osprey, an amber-list bird – produces three to five eggs per clutch, although, unlike the osprey, it often lays them in a nest comprising nothing more than a shallow scrape in the ground, concealed in the heather.

By seven o'clock on the morning of the second laying, Laird delivered a fish, then settled on the eggs as Lady flew off for breakfast. Although he had suffered a bad press so far, the previous year's male osprey, Eric, had proved erratic at the start of the season. He had improved, so there was time for Laird to turn things round. Rumour was rife that Laird had been spurned by another female bird, who had kicked him out of a nearby eyrie. And, after all, he was ten years old: surely he must have done all this before. Poor Laird did not deserve quite so many baseless, disapproving comments, but Lady's fans were protective of her.

By half past ten, Osprey Towers was picture-postcard perfect as Lady sat with her two eggs tucked snugly beneath her and Laird preened companionably nearby. He bent and twisted every which way to reach all his feathers, stimulating the uropygial, or preen, gland above the base of his tail that oiled them, made them weatherproof and kept them in top condition.

The weeks ahead involved a lot of sitting prior to hatching, which made them an ideal time for Lady to turn her attention to her plumage. Birds renew their feathers at different rates, once, twice or three times a year; the willow ptarmigan, for instance, moults three times each year to maintain its protective camouflage in the ever-changing sub-Arctic. Lady's long, strong wing and tail feathers generally lasted for a couple of years; her dark-pigmented feathers wore better than any white ones. This was quite economical, feather-wise.

Female ospreys shed and renew their worn feathers during the incubation period. Moulting is quite a demanding process for birds, but vital because feathers do not last for ever: they become weakened or damaged by flying, friction, the weather and parasites. It drains the bird's energy to grow new ones, involving heat loss when feathers are shed. When flight feathers moult, it can take even more effort to fly. Unlike most other birds, swans, ducks and geese lose all their flight feathers in one go, so, for a while, they can't fly at all. This is not so with the osprey, which moults its primary flight feathers in batches, working out to the wing tip; it stops moulting before it makes its marathon migration. Male ospreys never moult during the breeding season as they are too preoccupied with hunting.

That morning neither bird was busy; indeed, the pair

were the epitome of calm and contentment. It augured well, and the day when Lady's second egg appeared turned out to be a good one for ospreys everywhere: news came in of many eggs laid around the country. While every breeding season has its share of ups and downs, this was a day to treasure.

But over the next few weeks there would be some heart-in-the-mouth moments heralding potential disaster, which, in Lady's case, would be too cruel given that she had beaten the odds and completed her gruelling journey to Scotland to breed that spring. She did not have many cards left to play if the Fates conspired against her.

A few days later Lady sat tight on the nest during a cold, wet night, determined to keep her eggs warm despite the foul weather. Bedraggled and frozen in the driving rain, she was so exposed in her treetop eyrie that those watching her from the relative comfort of the Lowes hide felt guilty that they were dry. It was just after one in the morning, and the egg-protection team, from the army of osprey watchers that had formed since the laying of the first egg, were on red alert for egg number three.

Ospreys usually lay every two days, so it takes about five days to complete a clutch; 18 April was the likely date for the next egg. It had been a relatively sunny day with little wind but, by mid-afternoon, Lady was restless and uncomfortable. Later she began calling for Laird, who flew to the nest but left without seeming to understand what she wanted. She remained unsettled, grunting and shuffling, until early the following morning she stood up to reveal egg number three. It gave her a grand total of fifty-eight eggs laid over a lifetime, which was nothing short of a minor miracle.

Dawn on the nineteenth broke at about half past five, and light seeped over the hills, now draped in a white blanket. Heavy snow provided a dazzling, dramatic back-drop for Lady as she sat shivering on the nest at the end of a long night – a cold one on which to produce her last egg. It was up to Laird now to arrive with an early-morning fish to reward her effort, but when he showed up he had nothing to feed her. Eventually, Lady got up and stretched, stood on the edge of the nest, opened her wings and flew off, presumably to catch her own breakfast. Hopefully, Laird would take over the incubation, and avoid trampling the eggs as he had a tendency to do. The crust of ice crystals covering Lady's back, a scattering of sequins on a feathered ballgown, had only just melted.

Perhaps Lady would have more luck with hunting than Laird had experienced. The watchers also hoped that the third egg would hatch: it was much whiter than the first two, so there were concerns about its fertility. The power brokers of medieval Europe prized white birds, which were seen as enhancing their prestige; the same went for white eggs among collectors. Birds' eggs range from plain whites and blues to myriad other colours and markings. Osprey eggs are oval and roughly the size of a chicken's egg; the shell has a slight sheen and feels quite coarse. They are usually whitish, graduating towards a creamy yellow, pinkish-buff, spattered with bold chocolate- or reddish-brown spots and blotches.

Birds that lay their eggs in the open, like the osprey, or on the ground, like the merlin, rely on camouflage, either by coloured spotting, mottling or patterning so that they blend into the surrounding environment and are not easily seen by predators. Birds that lay their eggs in holes or anywhere poorly lit, such as the kingfisher in its deep burrow in the bank of a stream, are more likely to produce lighter, plainer eggs that are easy for the parent birds to locate in the dark.

The patterning and colouring of each bird's egg is unique. The eggs bear the female's own imprint, so it is possible to identify a bird from her eggs. When female cuckoos lay their eggs in the nests of other birds, they can match the unique shell patterning of the meadow pipits, dunnocks and reed warblers they dupe. That is a sort of skill, too, a cheats' charter.

Over the next five to six weeks Lady's three eggs required patient, diligent incubation; a good month or so in the moss-and-grass nest cup, tucked beneath her brood patch, a specific area of bare skin on the bird's breast that develops for incubation, a featherless hot spot. It is common to all birds, male and female, and dense with heat-generating blood vessels, which enable it to perform like a localized radiator. Brood patches are necessary because feathers are such good insulators that none of the adult's body heat, required to speed up development of the embryos, would reach the eggs without them. The feathers grow back after hatching.

By 20 April, Lady had been brooding her eggs for seven days. Using the Lowes thirty-seven-day incubation average, a quick calculation indicated that, provided all went well, the chicks were due to hatch in the second half of May; the first egg laid would be the first to hatch. The following morning was windy, and there was a heavy frost. Laird had arrived at dawn with a pike. Fishing conditions were better than they had been the previous day. He seemed to have developed a preference for pike, which were, evidently, abundant in the Lunan lochs, but sometimes caught perch and the odd trout. He began to deliver the latter towards the end of the month, inviting speculation that he was widening his hunting territory.

As incubation had got under way, Laird had finally proved himself as a hunter. He fished only occasionally on Loch of the Lowes. The nearby Loch of Butterstone had a fish farm, but Loch of Craiglush, the hill lochs to the north and the River Tay were all within easy range, as were a number of ponds. The birds' diet was rich in brown and rainbow trout, and pike, which bask near the surface of the water and are thus easier to catch than trout.

During incubation, the birds developed a daily routine. Lady grew impatient for food just after dawn. As soon as

Laird delivered a fish, he took over incubation while she flew off to feed on her preferred tree. He had got the hang of incubation and even appeared to enjoy taking a turn: sometimes he sat for up to two hours. He was taking his co-parenting duties seriously, a relief after his shaky start – but with some hard-to-please people he still couldn't win. On the Lowes osprey blog, the early jokes about him as a young whippersnapper or toyboy had developed into sneers about stay-at-home husbands and sensitive New Age men.

Sometimes there was work to be done when intruder birds or other animals turned up to threaten the nest. Ospreys give their distinctive warning alarm call, *kew-kew-kew*, if anything bothers them, such as a rival bird flying over or a human on the ground near their tree – this is one of the clues the egg-protection teams recognize in identifying intruders. Beneath the Lowes nest, deer sometimes grazed by the nesting tree, but that did not trouble Laird or Lady. Other birds did, especially if they flew too close to the nest, as some crows liked to do. Fending them off turned dangerous if a fight started in or around the nest.

In late April, there was a big drama when an unknown male osprey flew near it three times in one morning. He did not come close enough for watchers to identify him, but he got more than close enough, within fifty feet, for Laird to become upset and see him off. By early May, another male stranger landed on the nest, much to the fury of its occupants. Despite frantic mantling, squabbling and shouting on and near the nest, eggs and birds emerged unscathed.

But who was the intruder? Could it be Eric, returning late in the season?

This set alarm bells ringing, especially after news from another Scottish nature reserve had reminded everyone of how lucky they had been so far at Lowes with a relatively peaceful breeding season: an osprey nest had failed after a fight had broken out between two rival males. War had been waged over several days, and in a series of fierce skirmishes all three eggs were smashed or tipped out, one by one, by the intruder. All was not lost: the osprey pair retreated to a back-up nest, which resulted in the successful fledging of three chicks later that season.

A few years earlier, a similar but different drama had been enacted at that reserve at the start of the breeding season. The resident osprey female – who had successfully bred two chicks the previous year – had arrived back from migration and been joined by a male. The pair began mating. Two days later, feathers flew with the arrival of a second male; the subsequent fight for the female ousted the first. The drama now focused on the eggs, because no one could be sure which male bird was the father. Nifty arithmetic revealed that the right male was incubating them. But was he the male from the year before?

A CCTV link-up solved the mystery. When experts examined footage from both years they identified similar key head and eye-stripe markings on the incubating male, which told them he was the female's original mate. Sighs of relief all round.

These episodes were salutary reminders of what can go wrong. It was not enough for the birds to return from their epic migration, locate a good nest site, find and defend a nest, mate, lay eggs and settle. There was many a slip between laying and hatching, as became abundantly clear at Loch Garten, when a similar drama occurred between its established breeding pair, Henry and EJ. At Lowes, everyone wondered what might have happened if Eric had returned that year to find Lady with a new mate.

The weeks of incubation were relatively sedentary for the osprey pair at Lowes, as indeed they are for most ospreys. But they are wild birds, and must endure wild conditions, some of which involve the weather. One windy morning, towards the end of April, Lady was snugly lodged in her lofty eyrie, incubating the eggs. She looked secure enough, even though the tree was rocking. She had put up with worse, especially during the previous year's wild May gales after the chicks had hatched. The osprey architects had earned their stripes in 2009: the nest had withstood some ferocious Scottish weather. That winter, after the birds had left, one of Lowes' routine periodic nest inspections confirmed that the base was rock solid.

At least Laird seemed to be enjoying his duties as a husband. He kept himself busy with a spot of housework – and everyone else amused with his unstinting efforts at nest expansion, with his regular-as-clockwork deliveries of oversized sticks. The space for incubating was gradually decreasing, but the nest's high walls gave welcome shelter from the miserable weather. But he continued to bring more and more nest material. How would they all squeeze in once the chicks arrived?

All around the osprey there were signs of spring: the woods at Lowes had sprouted carpets of white wood anemone and sorrel; the meadows were pale yellow, bright with cowslips and primroses. Around the loch, willows and alders were in leaf, hawthorn and wild cherry in blossom and the sleepy old oaks in bud. In every corner of the reserve creatures were building. The woodland birds and red squirrels were busy making their nests and dreys, chasing and winning prospective mates. Greater spotted woodpeckers could be heard declaring their presence all day long with loud calling and their distinctive spring drumming displays; it was hoped new juveniles would arrive soon.

In the nest box, where the resident blue tits had made a snug home, the initial egg had been laid on 29 April, probably the first of half a dozen or so. The female would not start incubation until all the eggs were laid but the first eggs stayed safe and warm in the bedding in the box. It was not long, though, before she was incubating at least six; the male brought food for her to the nest.

Far out on the water, the loch birds had been indulging in their signature mating displays. Some of the mallards had ducklings already, which, within about ten hours of hatching, had been led to water to feed. A mallard's eggs hatch over a twenty-four-hour period, and the ducklings remain nest-bound just until they are dry and have grown accustomed to using their legs. The great crested grebes were nesting too. Soon it would be Lady's turn to show off her chicks.

By 10 May, there were just ten days left to go before the first osprey chick might hatch. The week before had seen a couple of minor incidents: Lady had damaged the talon on the second toe of her left foot, which needed to heal and re-grow before she started hunting again. For his part, Laird had excelled himself in the nest-building stakes by carrying in a big rock; presumably he had not been able to separate it from the useful clump of moss – perfect for the nest bowl – that he had spotted growing on it. That week his distinct dislike of the Canada geese that had settled too near the nest developed to the extent that he spent a Sunday endlessly dive-bombing one poor bird in the loch. Perhaps he was right to be so distrustful: by arriving first and breeding earlier than the osprey, Canada geese have been known to usurp osprey nests, although only when ospreys build them on the ground. After which no amount of dive-bombing or intimidation can persuade these geese to go.

Instead of a calm spell prior to hatching, another day of nest drama ensued when an un-ringed intruder male osprey began a campaign of harassment against Lady. She had started alarm-calling at half past four one morning to alert Laird and scare off the other bird. The intruder landed on the nest at one point, but Lady did a fine job of fighting him off without damage to herself or the eggs. The bird flew away but hung about over the next few days, coming and going, before eventually giving up.

The date for the earliest-possible hatching of Lady's first egg, 18 May, came and went. There was one certain sign of imminent chicks: Lady's refusal to leave her eggs to feed. Over the years a pattern had emerged: as hatching neared, she grew increasingly possessive of her eggs. This accounted for the fact that Laird had incubated the eggs only for short stints over the previous couple of days.

Also, Lady had started peering down into the nest bowl, as if she was listening to something deep within it. She had been doing this for a few days, and what she had heard was the sound of her chicks inside the shells. It is a sound all osprey females like to hear, a good sign that a chick is wriggling around, keen to get out. Lady's regular turning or rolling of all three eggs continued. She had begun fussing over them more and more, and often tilted her head to one side as she gazed down at them. Hopefully, there would be physical signs of hatching before long, a crack or a small hole, revealing the tiny hammer-like egg-tooth on a chick's beak that enables it to break free of the shell.

All the signs pointed to a first chick, yet the nest was abandoned again one late afternoon, after just five minutes' incubating by Laird, supposedly sitting in for Lady, who was away eating the fish he had just brought her. It was odd that, even as the first hatching drew ever nearer, the pair left the nest completely exposed to all comers. There had been two significant periods during incubation when the eggs had been abandoned: initially, soon after first laying, during a spell of very cold weather; again, when it was sunny and marginally warmer, but then the nest was left for about an hour, giving plenty of time for any opportunistic predators to strike, such as the ever-present crows, buzzards and gulls.

Lady's departure this time, on what was assumed to be the last lap of incubation, had been accompanied by her loud squealing to Laird as she flew off: 'Now just stay put till I get back!' But Laird was his own bird and carried on regardless, cheeping loudly, apparently to himself, before also flying off. The nest was uncovered for a matter of minutes, but it felt risky nonetheless, given the intermittent presence of that intruder male. Soon Laird was in trouble again with the Lowes osprey-blog posters, who had noted his absence with great displeasure. On his return he perched coolly near the nest in his favourite tree, preened a little, then took off to perform a fabulous aerial display.

Lady's resumption of her duties, turning her eggs before settling down on them, was met with a sigh of relief among the blog posters. Laird's apparent fecklessness was losing him friends left, right and centre. Some webcam watchers even began to switch off for a while because they could not bear the suspense; another blamed herself for a dream in which she had discovered that the eggs had been irretrievably abandoned. Another blogger, at the end of her tether, remarked on how that year was supremely disconcerting because, although the weather was now warm and the nest cosy, she could not recall Lady ever having been away from it so much before. She was sure she had not behaved like that with reliable Eric on board, and longed for her to revert to the great mother she usually was; any chick now, she added despairingly, would be a bonus.

It would indeed have been tragic to lose the eggs at this late stage, and fears were expressed that Lady might have sensed a problem with the eggs; it is known that if eggs fail the parent birds abandon them. That could be the only explanation because it was so unlike Lady to be away from the nest for so long. Occasional voices of calm intervened in this dismal exchange: there was no real cause for concern because, in this heat, the eggs were fine. Perhaps, also, the nest had not been targeted by an opportunist intruder because Lady was within sight of it.

Lady's ultimate return saw calm was restored. By the early evening of 19 May, peace reigned over a lovely but windy day's end. But the bloggers were still anxious, dreading Laird's arrival with a fish, not trusting him to sit on the eggs while Lady was gone. It was time for an early night as, one by one, the Lowes osprey-webcam army switched off their computers, hopeful of recovering their equilibrium for the next day's turbulent osprey drama – and that by the week's end there would be good news to share.

Tantalizingly, elsewhere at Lowes, on the morning of 19 May, the blue tit chicks had started to hatch. The previous year, they had done so on the same day as the osprey, so it felt like a good omen.

7 Beating the eggers

For Lady, at least, who did the biggest share of it, incubation meant sitting, but for egg collectors, or eggers, it meant precisely the opposite. Eggers are the outcasts of the bird-watching world, and egg collecting is a crime. Since 1997 Tayside Police has coordinated the nationwide Operation Easter, targeting the most determined of the egg thieves known to them and the RSPB.

The eggers' overall profile is haphazard, in that they live in a few random hotspots: Coventry, Merseyside and Devon; but rarely Scotland, and range widely across professions and social classes. But two things are constant: they are invariably men, and their numbers have been in decline. In 2003, the UK had about 300 active eggers; by 2010 the number had dropped to about twenty-five, probably because legislation is stricter, with the threat of a prison sentence, and is supported by greater police activity and nest protection.

A further constant yet initially surprising feature of the egg collectors' profile is that they are often accomplished field ornithologists. Indeed, there was a time, not far distant, when naturalists and bird lovers were as keen as today's eggers to add yet more beautiful, desirable eggs to their extensive collections. In the nineteenth and twentieth centuries a great deal of ornithological fieldwork was done regularly by shooting the birds and taking their eggs. Specimen and egg collectors were not always on the wrong side of the law: in the cases of avid Victorian collectors, like naturalist Charles Darwin and zoologist Walter Rothschild, they often did so with the law's blessing and in the name of science.

The Natural History Museum at Tring was founded in 1892 as Rothschild's private museum, in which ultimately, among his vast collection, there were two hundred thousand birds' eggs and three hundred thousand bird skins (plus more than two million butterflies and moths and 144 giant tortoises). Rothschild had spent his boyhood and youth collecting birds and other animals, and studying wildlife. Darwin was a keen collector of insects in his early youth and spent a great deal of time hunting and shooting, before he embarked on his long and world-changing collecting career.

Before it became illegal, many people enjoyed collecting eggs for interest and fun, including, in the mid-twentieth century, the esteemed British naturalist Bill Oddie. In a newspaper magazine feature in 2010, he expressed his lack of regret at having been a teenage egg collector. It had given him a good grounding in birdsong and behaviour, as well as the patience everyone needs if they want to have anything to do with wildlife.

Today things are different. In March 2002 – when ospreys were a controlled species with only 140 breeding pairs in Scotland – police seized a clutch of osprey eggs, probably stolen from a Scottish nest, in an Operation Easter initiative. Operation Easter has secured other convictions over the years, including a repeat collector sentenced to four months' imprisonment. His spell in jail gave him the dubious honour of being the first person imprisoned under the Countryside and Rights of Way (CRoW) Act 2000. The Lowes reserve is well protected against wildlife crime, as are most of the public sites. They all use new technology now and keep one step ahead of the wildlife criminals. But the real deterrent has been stricter penalties. A fine for stealing a single osprey egg can be as much as £5,000.

The number of eggers may be falling, but a hard core remains. Some diehards are so obsessed that not even the threat of a prison sentence puts them off. Take the case of one egg collector, once listed as the UK's most wanted, who saw himself as a lover of nature and considered osprey watchers overly sentimental. The core of his argument in his own defence was that he targeted only the freshest eggs so that the birds had time to lay another clutch; ornithological research shows that the later laying of a clutch results in later-developing chicks that are less likely to thrive, on migration especially.

This egger's *raison d'être* was to rediscover the initial excitement he had felt as a schoolboy raider of nests. Like any addict, he needed to get his fix: the rush of adrenalin that capturing the quarry gave him. The challenge was to have something nobody else had. He was a trophy hunter on a par with Victorian big-game hunters. He was hooked, too, on the forbidden thrill of secret, meticulous planning and plotting – preparing maps, assembling specialist climbing gear, elaborate escape routes. It was real-life SAS-style endurance and adventure, which involved miles of walking, often at night, swimming across icy lochs, abseiling down cliff faces, sleeping rough and surviving extreme conditions. The eggs were the icing on the cake. In 2001, crushed by a catalogue of convictions and keen to avoid jail, he gave himself up, along with his two decades' worth of field knowledge and his egg collection, in return for the removal of his name from the police database. Among the 1,500 eggs he surrendered were those of the osprey.

Eggers treat egg collecting like a military operation. Once they pick a nest site, they plan their raid in advance down to the very last detail to ensure that they get it right. If they are caught, their climbing gear is impounded with their means of transport. It is difficult to prove a nest source, especially if eggers are caught a couple of years down the line, but, luckily for law enforcement, a lot of egg collectors keep careful written records as well as video footage and photographs of themselves stealing the eggs. Several have been jailed since the CRoW 2000 and the Criminal Justice (Scotland) Act 2003 came into force, often on the basis of their own scrupulous record-keeping. On one occasion, during a house raid in which dead birds were found in the freezer, a trophy album of photographs, featuring eggs, nests and nest sites, was confiscated. This sad booty belonged to a man who liked to talk with some emotion about the exquisite look and feel of a bird's wing. He was sentenced to four months in prison.

A BBC radio documentary on egg collectors, *We Are the Egg Men*, included a reading from the detailed field diary of a prolific and notorious egg collector, Colin Watson, who, perhaps with some sense of divine retribution, had died by falling out of a tree on an egg raid. It told of one visit he had made to Loch Ness, which involved a tricky ascent up a hundred-foot tree to an osprey nest. His diary gave precise details of his trip, including a stop-and-search encounter with police. Most egg collectors record their 'work' meticulously, noting exact arrivals and departures – of men and birds – weather conditions, how many eggs were taken and who took them; they also cross-reference eggs. Their diaries bizarrely mirror serious scientific work, such as the remarkable records of pioneering eighteenth-century British naturalist cleric Gilbert White, the patron saint of amateur field naturalists, or RSPB field-research trips.

But there is a different end-game. Eggers take the eggs

home and blow any burgeoning life out of them through a pinprick hole in the shell. They rinse and store them in a sterile glass display case, closed drawer or lock-up garage, and presumably gloat over them from time to time. This is precisely what nineteenth-century egg collectors had done, although their collections were legal and exhibited with some trumpeting in impressive baronial halls and country manor houses. Lewis Dunbar, a professional egger of the time, who collected for Charles St John among others, carried out many of his raids at the scenic ruined castle-tower eyrie on the island at Loch an Eilein, and famously rinsed the shells of the eggs he took with whisky (having reportedly walked miles through a snowstorm and swum hundreds of yards through the chilly waters of the loch to reach them). There were many like him, now long forgotten, such as the then well-known English egg collector John Wolley, who bought some of Dunbar's eggs, and sportsman and trophy hunter Roualeyn George Gordon-Cumming, the second son of a Scottish baronet, an inveterate wildlife collector, particularly celebrated as a lion hunter.

The result is that those eggs never hatched and that bird never reproduced. For anyone monitoring the nest, in the way that raptor-study workers do, or indeed any wildlife conservationist, this is nothing short of a disaster. For ospreys, in particular, there have been more than a hundred nest robberies since they recolonized Scotland. The birds would have a much wider range in the UK and would have colonized England much sooner than they have done if none of this had happened.

The osprey would not have rallied so well without conservationists, who provided nest protection during the breeding season to combat egg theft. In the early days osprey watch was mostly about keeping a log of nest events seen through high-power binoculars with a few hide comforts such as a portable gas ring for hot drinks plus the odd blanket or rug. Roy Dennis recalls a voluminous Russian bearskin coat kept in the hide at Loch Garten in the 1960s, where osprey watch started, as Operation Osprey, and provided a training ground for new conservationists.

Just before the launch of the 2010's osprey watch, Emma Rawling took over as that year's Perthshire ranger. Part of her remit, in a tradition going back twenty years, was to coordinate the twenty-four-hour nest-protection watch, once any eggs were laid. It was the main thing she felt she could do to help the osprey thrive.

Early observation hides were often improvised lookouts made from bits of wood and sacking. Scottish RSPB's George Waterston recalled how, in the 1950s at Loch Garten, he had to crawl into one because the hessian roof sagged so low. Once inside he sat 'on a box, in extreme discomfort, peering out through a small slit in the sacking in front of the hide'. Early equipment was unsophisticated too, largely reliant on microphones fixed to the nest tree linked to a loudspeaker in the observation hide. These Heath Robinson-style alarm systems, which were tripped by anyone climbing the tree, were not entirely successful, due to the ease with which foraging red squirrels triggered them. The use of practical deterrents such as swathing the trunk in barbed or razor wire remain standard, as does chopping off lower limbs to make climbing harder – although this is useless against eggers wearing spiked, lumberjack-style boots.

Later, innovations included infra-red beams, pressure pads and electronic warning systems, which often fell foul of the wildlife that nibbled through wires. Deer that browsed on the alder and other forest trees were frequently picked up by the microphone and mistaken for human predators. In any case, technology is only as good as the person watching it.

During the four years that Roy Dennis was warden of RSPB Loch Garten in the 1960s, when eggers were highly active and anti-egger equipment was extremely basic, not one egg was lost. He attributed this largely to his vigilant team of egg guardians. According to Mike Everett, who oversaw the recruitment of volunteer wardens in the pioneer days of nest protection at Loch Garten, they ranged from local grandmothers to fervent Marxist students and visitors from overseas. In Mark Cocker and Richard Mabey's *Birds Britannia*, he describes how he had to find about nine wardens each week during the sixteen-week breeding season, a total of some 150 watchers. To accommodate everyone, a cold-water encampment of canvas-and-pole tents grew up, a Spartan lifestyle made bearable by the sense of worth that the project gave to everyone – with endless games of Scrabble, late-night talk and laughter, coffee and cigarettes in the mess caravan.

Frank Hamilton, who retired in 1994 as director of RSPB Scotland, a post he had held for fifteen years, remembers the makeshift conditions at Loch Garten. In 1959, after a successful hatching, he spent two months there with his new wife. She found herself cooking in a rickety caravan with two burners for up to ten campers who were helping to protect the nest.

Osprey watch started at Lowes after attempts had been made at egg theft once it had become known that ospreys were trying to nest there. It has a long-standing volunteer network, with the same people coming back each year to do a stint – not the Gordon Highlanders now but a dedicated band that includes photographer Kevin Hacker, whose photograph of Lady appears on the cover of this book.

At Lowes there are always two guardians on duty. One person watches the cameras from inside the visitor centre while the other is out in an observation hide, using old-fashioned fieldcraft: if somebody approaches the nest the wild animals in and around the reserve will announce their presence. Deer bark, ducks quack and geese honk long before any human gets too close to the tree. Fieldcrafters use their eyes and ears; they know which lights are normal or if a poacher is around with a lamp. Such full-on, hands-on care is necessary, despite the osprey's legal protection and acknowledged rarity: the last recorded osprey egg theft in Scotland took place on Speyside in 2009, and in Perthshire seven years earlier.

Although osprey watch starts from the time the eggs are laid, it does not end precisely when they hatch. There is an extension of the daylight watch for two weeks or so after hatching until the chicks have passed their really vulnerable stage. Any human presence may scare off the female, who may leave the nest and circle overhead for half an hour, long enough for the chicks to get cold and die.

At Lowes, osprey watch is seasonal, but the reserve remains open all year round with wildlife's ever-changing presence throughout the seasons. In autumn, there are bat walks and talks. Of the eighteen species of bat in the UK, seventeen are known to breed there, among them the common pipistrelle, soprano pipistrelle, Daubenton's, brown long-eared, Natterer's and noctule bats. Red squirrels take centre stage too, but are elusive. The birds that flock to Lowes in the wintertime are sometimes more reliable, especially the greylag goose, an amber-list bird, ancestor of most domestic geese and largest of the wild geese that are native to Europe and the UK.

The wintering flocks at Lowes of these truly wild birds are especially appealing: there are sometimes up to 3,000 greylag roosting on the loch, with a similar number of common and black-headed gulls. The gulls were often still there when the osprey returned in spring, and osprey watch began. The osprey guardians often heard them calling, bickering, all night long.

Lowes has experienced no problems with nest-egg theft for a few years, but they feel it is wise to keep up their vigilance. In 1995 an infra-red camera, microphone and television monitor were added to their defensive arsenal. The new equipment recorded no human disturbance during that incubation period but revealed a few pine martens around the base of the tree at night. Pine martens belong to the mustelid, or weasel, family, which also includes the stoat, otter, polecat and badger. Those seen at Lowes were the first recorded members of the species for the reserve, although they had been spotted previously in the vicinity. Pine martens, like the osprey, were once heavily persecuted, so much so that Scotland's woodlands are their last UK stronghold.

Peter Ferns was involved in wildlife watching and conservation before he became Lowes' visitor-centre manager. He undertook the first of many osprey watches at the observation hide the same year the new equipment was installed. All those years in the hide, watching the birds' every movement, have deepened his already strong attachment to the osprey and Lady in particular. To him they were wild birds, and he was not precious about them, but his contact with them made him feel he had got to know them.

His first memory of Lady was of her covered with snow as she incubated her eggs in 1995; she successfully reared three chicks. Even a spell of fierce wintry conditions could not stop her. Inside the hide it was often cold, sometimes several degrees below freezing, but Ferns remembers the fun between the two volunteers on night shift, often joking around to keep warm and awake. He was alone one night when he found a novel way to keep going by writing a story about a hedgehog for his kids. At the end of his shift, he took it home, put it on the kitchen table and went straight to bed. When he got up, he found that his wife had lovingly typed it up. It was a bedtime favourite with his kids for years. As a volunteer, latterly, Peter Ferns worked every weekend at Lowes, doing osprey watch and wildlife count. His wife and children were involved for a while, but the children stopped when they became teenagers; Ferns thinks they will come back to it in the future, that it is in their blood.

Over the years Ferns has experienced numerous run-ins with eggers, and they make his blood boil. One memorable encounter took place at four o'clock one morning, just after Lady had laid a clutch of eggs at the start of a new breeding season. Ferns was on duty with a fellow volunteer when heavy footsteps on the boardwalk leading up to the observation hide alerted them to the presence of someone outside. It was out of tourist hours, long past the time for idle curiosity. The megawatt beam of the torch they shone into the darkness picked out a group of men in camouflage gear. Ferns summoned his full height and deepest voice to ask what they wanted. That was a formality: he knew precisely why they were there. He could not accuse them of anything, though, because they had done nothing wrong. And, although their military-style appearance might have been a giveaway, there is no telltale eggers dress code: some don Gore-Tex and balaclavas, buckles and boots; others just pull on jeans and T-shirts. The police know who the eggers are and keep nature reserves like Lowes up to date with identifying details, such as car number-plates and names.

Peter Ferns established that those men's cars had been noticed in the car park a few times and were on the police list. But no professional egger would have turned up at the Lowes hide at four a.m. True pros case the joint, visit out of season, learn the lie of the land, and the times, day and night, when the least number of people are likely to be there. They visit during the day, just like any reserve visitor, to see how things work. The egg collectors Peter Ferns disturbed were most likely amateurs in egg-collection crime. Once the men, who were just chancers, saw the reserve was so well protected, they did not even consider making an attempt and left. Which is the major purpose and ultimate triumph of osprey watch.

Many eggers go for unprotected nest sites, like the one a wildlife crime officer saw from his hideout among the heather of a Perthshire hillside, alerted by the haunting cries of an osprey, which sounded to him like the keening of a grieving mother. The bird was telling him her eggs had gone, calling constantly as she flew above and around her empty nest, distraught.

In the 1980s, the RSPB's Investigations Section instigated the Wildlife Crime Officers (WCO) network, a web of police officers, of which this man was a member. They were initially known as Wildlife Liaison Officers and tasked by their forces with handling wildlife crime. Tayside Police's Operation Easter and the RSPB also put in traditional fieldcraft to help guard Scotland's nesting ospreys in their most vulnerable periods. Sometimes dedicated, hardy groups of guardians spent days and nights on the hills, walking, watching and waiting, in bothies and makeshift hides, prepared for the worst. They tried everything to keep the osprey safe and deter egg theft, even painting nest trees with weather-durable DNA liquid to help identify anyone who climbed them (the first wildlife conviction using DNA profiling was in 1993). But for that WCO on his remote Perthshire hillside, and those like him, the point of their patrols across rural landscapes was to look after what was there today – or it might not be there tomorrow.

So egg theft is on the decline – but there is a new and increasing problem of what the law calls 'reckless disturbance'. In one instance on Mull, an Aberdeen photographer spent too long near a white-tailed eagle's nest, trying to get the perfect photograph and thereby unsettling the nesting pair during incubation. Reported by Mull Eagle Watch to local police, he was fined £600 in the first successful prosecution for reckless disturbance of sea eagles.

It is not just organized bird-protection watches that ensure wild birds do not fall victim to wildlife crime. Some dedicated individuals take on the egg thieves too, among them wildlife artist, nest-builder and bird ringer Keith Brockie, who has been waging war against them for decades. One year, at the end of his tether over an osprey pair's persistent failure to breed because of continual egg theft, he contacted 45 Commando Royal Marines, who used all their strong-arm capability to call a halt to it. Coincidentally, Simon Milne, now chief executive of the Scottish Wildlife Trust, was serving with 45 Commando (as Adjutant) at that time and he coordinated and approved the task following the request from Brockie. The commandos were well equipped with the latest night-sight and other specialist equipment and their involvement led to a thief being apprehended. This was at the time of the first Gulf War, and the *Scotsman* ran a cartoon captioned 'Mr Bush send in Troops'. with a drawing of Mrs Thatcher speaking on the phone and saying, 'I am sorry Mr President, all our crack troops are guarding an osprey nest in Perthshire'. The original hangs in Milne's flat in Edinburgh and is a nice link between his career as a Royal Marine then and now a conservationist.

But the power and might of military training is not always put to good use, especially when vast riches beckon. In August 2010 Jeffrey Lendrum, a former member of the Rhodesian SAS, received a thirty-month jail sentence for trying to smuggle out of Britain the rare peregrine eggs he had stolen from a nest on a mountainside in Wales. In contravention of UK export restrictions, and despite a ban on wild-falcon importation by the United Arab Emirates, where those eggs were heading, the eggs of these wild birds are highly sought after and command high prices. Those Lendrum stole were worth £70,000 and destined for the black market in Dubai, where falconry is popular.

One commonly mistaken belief about the band of egger brothers is that they do it for the money. Often they do not: they frequently keep the eggs. But this man, at least, broke the mould. Lendrum, who pleaded guilty at his trial, was described as a serial 'wildlife criminal' and used dare-devil tactics to steal eggs, once abseiling off a cliff, another time lowering himself from a helicopter to attain his goal. He had been arrested at the airport, en route to Dubai, because of his suspicious behaviour in the business-class lounge where he was seen darting in and out of the shower. He was discovered to have fourteen peregrine eggs wrapped in socks and bandaged to his body as a makeshift incubator. The unhatched eggs were entrusted to an experienced falconer to incubate, after which eleven hatched. New nest sites for the peregrine chicks were found in Scotland. It was a triumph over wildlife criminals and a key victory for conservationists.

When police had searched Lendrum's properties, they had found equipment for egg collecting, including incubators, a GPS system and walkie-talkies. It was one of the most serious incidents of illegal egg collecting for decades. But if Lendrum and his like were dedicated to wildlife crime, consorting with a greedy, obsessive demi-monde, they faced an increasingly determined international community, fired up by a more positive passion for the birds. Fortunately, like those eleven falcons, the osprey are also beating the eggers.

8 One day in the life

Lady would often be half awake in the early evening as she sat amid the forest in her lofty, perennially blue-green Scots pine eyrie high above the loch. She only tucked her head down later, to sleep when it suited her best. As May progressed, the nights at Lowes were getting shorter, and it did not get dark until after ten.

As Lady settled for the night, other animals were stirring, with hedgehogs on their nightly forages for the beetles, caterpillars, earthworms, slugs and snails that are their favourite food, and deer roaming the loch shore and even staking a nocturnal claim to the Lowes car park. Tawny owls were often to be heard calling, away from their daytime woodland roost sites, and one was seen catching a mouse near to a reserve bird feeder.

On 19 May, the night before the first chick was due, Lady joined them in their night-time bustle, as, ever restless, she was up and down throughout the small hours: up checking the eggs, down shuffling back into position. In nature's good time, hatching would happen.

It was going to be a long night, in the middle of which, at around three, a Canadian blogger heard Lady calling, a haunting *kew-kew-kew*, across the inky darkness of the loch, turning her head from side to side, as if on the lookout for something. An hour or so later, the sun was peeping over the horizon, casting its optimistic golden glow over mother bird and nest.

Dawn is a magical time for wildlife – when even Lowes' resident otter, a fish-eater like the osprey, is sometimes seen popping up above the surface of the loch, working the stretch of water between the observation hide and the osprey nest, hunting and fishing. One very early morning there was an unusual sighting of an eider, the UK's fastest-flying yet heaviest duck (amber-listed); it is a true sea duck, rarely far from coasts, where its liking for coastal molluscs has driven mussel farmers to distraction.

At that time of year, the sun rose due east over the loch from Lowes' visitor centre, bathing it in a rainbow of colours and dazzling shafts of light. It was turning into a glorious morning. At around six thirty, Laird delivered Lady's breakfast, a substantial, headless fish, which she flew off to enjoy. He had seemed to approach the nest almost tentatively that morning, and he and Lady had engaged in a careful changeover. Like Lady, he was restless and on high alert around the eggs.

Throughout the nights since the eggs had been laid, the Lowes staff, including the two species-protection officers and a sprinkling of dedicated volunteers, had been working the osprey-watch graveyard shift. They had been on night watch for more than a month now, and the consensus among them was that the first chick was most likely to hatch during daylight hours. In their view this was the most common time for hatching, although no one was sure if that was more by luck than design. Among many creatures, big and small, early morning is a favoured time for birth: the light maximizes the chance of survival, with, in the chicks' case, the chance to dry out and be fed.

Just before seven, rumours began to stir with reports of an evident crack in one of the eggs; amusingly, too, the egg had begun to move, rocking from side to side, end to end, in the nest bowl. The new life within was testing the measure of things before the great escape. With all that activity inside the shell, it was no wonder that neither parent bird could settle. There was also a tiny egg-tooth hole, although hatching could take several hours yet, depending on how strong the chick was. At this stage, the only real power it had lay in its neck, which added necessary muscle to the egg tooth that enabled it to pierce the shell.

Lady had been away from the nest for an unprecedented couple of hours, her absence perhaps explained by her awareness that this might be her last chance of relative freedom for a while. Once the first chick hatched, she would be on virtual permanent guard – and feeding duties – on the nest and loath to leave it. Eventually, on the nest again, Lady behaved much like any expectant parent in the final stages before birth: pacing around the nest edge, flapping her wings, tidying and engaging in last-minute home improvements, rearranging sticks or twigs from near the nest bowl to the outer edges, making space. She positioned herself briefly on the eggs but soon got up, turning them with her bill or her talons, using the inside of her foot, then lowering herself like an opening umbrella over them again. It was all going to plan.

By ten, the crack was substantial, and it was exciting, emotional, compulsive to watch the chick chip its way out with its egg tooth. Using the sharp, horny tooth like a small, spiky hammer to strike the shell, the little bird rotated inside, determined to be free. It came mini-beak first, then head, neck, wings, body – and, heave-ho, I'm out. Each stage of pushing had been followed by a pause for rest before more energetic wriggling, pushing, pushing, pushing, shrugging off the shell until finally the baby osprey fell face down into the nest, with no strength to hold up its floppy, one-size-too-big head, taking short breaths, a bird on the threshold of life. Welcome to the world, little osprey. Someone already had a name for it: Hope.

It was mid-morning, and the human squeals of delight for once drowned the choral symphony of the birds. Staff, volunteers and visitors who had been watching the hatching via the osprey-nest webcam footage whooped for joy at the arrival of the first chick to hatch at Lowes that season. With astonishingly accurate, fortuitous timing, an RAF fly-past roared across the skies in an unwitting yet fitting tribute to the tiny miracle of birth that had just taken place below.

The engines briefly fazed Lady, who had been tirelessly attentive as she kept vigil over her chick's birth struggle. Sometimes it can take a chick more than twenty-four hours to break out of the shell; most hatch within a day or two of pipping, or cracking, their shells. Osprey parents tend not to help but may break the shell by chance with their bill or feet. Towards the end of the hatching, Lady had gently nudged off a scrap of shell that covered the chick like an oversize hat; her feet, so menacing, looked huge as she walked carefully around the chick and remaining eggs, talons drawn in.

The chick's feet were the same bluish-grey as hers and its claws long and black, also like Lady's; this was the colour they would stay. No standing on them for the moment, although the chick would be mobile in about ten days' time. For the moment, it lay motionless, tiny, weak and helpless, doubtless exhausted after its exhilarating effort. A good rest was in order, even before first feeding.

Osprey young emerge from the egg semi-precocial, as do other birds of prey. The zoological term describes the way in which the young of some animals are able to move about and feed independently soon after hatching or birth. To a degree, the chick was able to do some of this. It had arrived in the world covered almost entirely with down, and its eyes would open within a few hours. It would be able to feed directly from Lady's bill. It would be a good few hours before it had dried out and managed to hold up its head, but it took only that time for it to turn from a bedraggled scrap to a more recognizably cute and fluffy baby bird. It would soon seem incredible that it had ever fitted inside the shell that had been its home for thirty-seven days. The shell itself would gradually disintegrate into the moss-and-grass centre of the nest or be scattered around the edges.

Remarkable, in a different way, was how easy it was to watch the chick's arrival, worldwide, live, via the wondrous osprey-nest webcam. Hatchings like this had previously been seen almost exclusively on specialist film and TV wildlife documentaries. This live webcam hatching highlighted the huge advances that had been made since the 1950s and 1960s when the osprey had first come back to breed. It was impossible in the early days to know for sure whether the eggs had been laid without climbing up the tree; then, everything around hatching and so much else was guesswork. In the decades that followed, at protected sites, a look inside the nest bowl was impossible because most nesting trees were wrapped in concertina razor wire to protect them from egg collectors.

At Loch Garten in the 1950s, the exact incubation period, even with a specialist parabolic-reflector microphone positioned beneath the nest, was hard to estimate. An article from around that time by George Waterston in

Bird News described how the first sign of one chick's hatching was a strange, deep grunting, a sort of *tyuck-tyuck-tyuck*, which came from the chick in response to its mother's warning *kew-kew-kew* (all of which could be heard on earphones and was recorded by the BBC Natural History Unit). It was a few days later that the first regular, high-pitched cheeping of the young bird was heard and a day or so after that before the mother could be seen feeding her chick.

The adult birds' feeding patterns change after hatching, with the female bird reluctant to leave the young. The male delivers his catch straight to the nest without stopping off beforehand to feed himself; post-hatching, Lady would eat on the nest – rather than taking the fish away to a feeding tree – tearing off morsels for the chicks, her head dipping down low into the nest to feed them. Sometimes tiny round heads would be seen popping up on wobbly, skinny necks, as the nestlings – the name for any young bird not yet old enough to leave the nest – reached towards Lady's bill to feed.

When chicks hatch, they are covered with short, thick buff down that resembles fur. This is replaced about ten to twelve days later by a charcoal-grey second down, which is woolly and dense and lasts for ten to fifteen days. At this stage they enter a reptilian stage, during which, for all the world, they resemble baby dinosaurs, appearing black and scaly. Feathers start to replace the down when they are about two weeks old, and the young birds have their first

115

complete set of feathers at about six weeks. They are generally a little paler and more spotted or speckled above than the full adult plumage they have at eighteen months old. The down is not waterproof so the chicks must be kept warm and dry under their mother.

Osprey chicks generally open their eyes just hours after hatching. Even then the osprey's signature black eye stripe is obvious. Now, like many newborns, for the next few days Lady's chick needed to spend a great deal of its time sleeping, as well as feeding little and often on tiny scraps of fish. The scar from the umbilical attachment to the yolk sac that had fed the chick as an embryo, visible along its belly, would soon fade. A chick's crop develops as it grows, bulging and distinctive in its scrawny neck when full of food. Without this pouch-like enlargement of the gullet, seen in many birds, in which food is stored and prepared for digestion, the chicks would need far more frequent feeding than they get.

While all this is easy to see now, it still feels like a privilege to watch the birds via webcams from Scotland to Montana; even when birds on the UK side of the Atlantic are asleep, it is possible to watch those nesting on the other side of the ocean – although there is a night camera at Lowes for the truly dedicated. For some people, such daily proximity to the birds makes them feel part of their lives. For one Lowes osprey-blogger, leaving home to go to work had been hard with hatching imminent – she joked that she was thinking of applying for maternity leave. A class of forty three- and four-year-olds in a Glasgow nursery who watched the hatching were subsequently appointed by Lowes as honorary aunties and uncles to Lady's new chick.

Great emotion followed the little bird's struggle into the world. Some described themselves on the osprey blog as over the moon, so excited that they could burst. There were tears, too, even from the chaps, one dismissing himself as a big Jessie. But for all those who had been following Lady's progress and her new breeding season at Lowes, it was a milestone moment. The spirit of camaraderie among the osprey bloggers was heart-warming and often hilarious. They were united in their passionate goodwill for Lady and for the other nesting birds whose progress many of them followed around the world. Like many a happy family, there was lots of teasing, of each other, and especially of Laird, taking him to task, although, secretly, at last, they were warming to him.

What especially united everyone that morning was the joyous realization of how well things had gone at Lowes that new osprey breeding season. Nest failures are most commonly caused by adverse weather conditions, food shortage, inexperience of birds nesting for the first time and, occasionally, egg collectors robbing the nest. There is no guarantee that just because an egg is laid a healthy chick will later emerge; sometimes eggs fail – infertile – or a recently hatched bird will not survive beyond its first few hours or days.

Lowes had suffered its share of sorrow on that count, and notably, three years earlier, when an osprey chick had died eight days after hatching. It had been one of three hatched that spring, from an egg laid on Easter Monday. Lowes staff on osprey watch could only observe helplessly as it died in the nest at five in the morning on 31 May. It had been the youngest and smallest of the three chicks, and it had just faded away. For Peter Ferns the death was not only a blow to osprey conservation but also an upsetting loss for him as it was hard not to form an attachment to the chicks. But nature can be cruel, as he acknowledged; at the end of the day, it is always survival of the fittest.

In a highly competitive nest, the chicks fight for attention and food, and it is frequently the largest and loudest that receive the lion's share. Fortunately, the surviving chicks that year were strong and active, despite some foul weather. It is acknowledged that the birds breed more successfully when the weather is good at key times in the breeding cycle. Bad weather had contributed to the chick's death.

All was well so far three years on at Lowes, but no one felt complacent. There was already stark evidence of what might happen at the Derby Cathedral nest site in the East Midlands, where a peregrine pair had just lost their second chick, its sad decline recorded on the cathedral's peregrine project webcams. The female peregrine had done what she could to help her weakling, sheltering it from the sun, feeding it, brooding over it, but in the end it had died. Although the outcome was depressing, it had been a chance to witness nature at work: often delightful, sometimes distressing but always salutary.

Everyone was hopeful that the falcon pair would continue to raise the remaining chicks into the magnificent birds they should become (although it is not the fastest bird in level flight, the peregrine can reach speeds of more than 150 mph during its spectacular stoops). One of the things that the osprey and the peregrine have in common is that they are the only diurnal birds of prey (active during the day) to range so widely around the globe and still be considered a single species.

The peregrines had roosted and hunted from that cathedral tower over the ages until, in the middle of the twentieth century, their numbers crashed. The pesticide DDT was established as the problem, causing eggshell thinning and reproductive failure. With the banning of DDT and the designation of the falcon, like the osprey, as a protected species, peregrine numbers began to rise again; by 2010, the falcon was green-listed as a bird of low conservation concern.

Britain's ospreys, like Sweden's, and unlike the peregrine, had never shown any consistent reproductive failure due to pesticides, possibly because most nested in areas where few pesticides were used. In fact, most European ospreys escaped the pesticide crash because their main feeding habitats were rarely sprayed or treated directly. In the United States it was a different matter. Of all the toxins, organochlorine compounds are the ones that have caused the osprey most harm, and proof that ospreys were accumulating organochlorines, such as DDT, first came to light in North America during the mid-1960s after the osprey population, on the north-east coast in particular, started to plummet during the 1950s and 1960s. DDT was seen as the answer to insect-borne disease, but the fish the osprey ate became contaminated with its toxic residues. In the 1970s, once the role of pesticides in their decline had been established, the birds began to make a good recovery. Steps were taken to limit the use of such chemicals, especially over marshes and other wetlands. The biggest osprey losses, along the north-east coast – where breeding numbers dropped by as much as 90 per cent – were probably due to direct DDT spraying of the salt marshes that were the osprey's feeding grounds.

In 1962 Rachel Carson's *Silent Spring* brought the effects of pesticide use to the world's attention, as well as introducing the importance of ecology into popular consciousness, creating fresh public awareness of the environment, which led to government policy changes and inspired the modern ecological movement. She exposed the destruction of wildlife through the widespread use of toxic chemicals, such as pesticides, fungicides and herbicides: entire US counties and whole states were sometimes sprayed against pests like the red ant.

In Britain, in spring 1961, the use of toxic chemicals on the land led to a countryside of dead or dying birds; tens of thousands were mown down by toxic spraying, often suffering painfully slow, agonizing deaths. It became linked, too, to premature human births and low birth-weights; later, children exposed to DDT in the womb had developmental problems. DDT was banned in Britain and the US in the 1970s, although in 2006, more than thirty years later, a study by the University of California, Berkeley, revealed that DDT is still detectable in 5–10 per cent of people, while DDE, into which it downgrades, is detectable in nearly everyone. It is still used against malaria-carrying mosquitoes in some countries.

In spring 2010, one mid-May Tuesday, the weather at Lowes had gone from snow with an Arctic wind, when it had felt like late autumn, to bright sunshine the following day. These were unsettling weather conditions, and es-pecially so for the osprey, not long back from tropical West Africa. But the weather had turned glorious for the first hatching on 20 May; it was hoped that it would remain so over the coming days when the other two eggs were expected to hatch – but nothing could be taken for granted, even though the reserve had an excellent track record for breeding. Since 1969, when the first osprey pair returned there, to the end of 2010's breeding season, sixty-eight chicks had been raised successfully on the site, forty-eight of which were Lady's.

All over Britain, hatchings were happening. It was generally a joyful time but at Lowes it had been quite a day: Lady's latest chick was not alone in being new to the world.

Lowes' blue tits had got in on the act too, with almost all of their eggs hatching; five chicks were hungrily gaping for food, and the adult birds were doing an excellent job of keeping them well supplied.

After all the excitement of the morning, spirits were still high, although everyone was exhausted, glad to have welcomed another healthy osprey chick into the world and relieved that the hatching had gone so smoothly. As the first chick to hatch, it probably had the best chance of survival, coming from what is usually the largest egg and, of course, having a head start over its nestlings.

And Laird was shaping up, bringing in no less than five fish to the nest throughout that first day. Perhaps it was time to give him the benefit of the doubt, and thank heaven that his paternal instincts seemed to be kicking in.

By late evening, there was already talk of names. Someone suggested 7Y1 (after Laird, who was ringed 7Y; with 7Y2 and 7Y3, hopefully, to follow). Giving the birds human names was a contentious issue: they were wild birds, not pets, and naming them might erode their wildness and potentially their dignity. At Lowes, they do not officially have a name for their star female osprey, partly because she has acquired so many over the years on different forums (beyond Lowes' control) so they cannot please everyone.

Peter Ferns, like many others who work closely with ospreys and other wildlife, is of the view that birds should not be given pet names or be turned into personalities. He had always referred to Lady simply as 'our female', but there was pressure to do otherwise; now he thinks of her given name, Lady of the Loch, as more of a title, one that was shortened to Lady. With the huge surge of public interest in their ospreys, it was a change that was difficult to resist.

At Lowes, Laird is known as green 7Y, after his ring colour and number, which is the route that scientists and experts like those at Lowes and Roy Dennis usually take. It does not help in involving the public, though. Any desire to engage the wider population in conservation – of ospreys or any wild animal – works best by naming the subjects so that people are able to identify easily with them. They feel excluded if the birds are referred to scientifically. Once local schools, especially, had become more involved with ospreys and osprey conservation, everything began to change; even Dennis had a 'named' osprey on his patch – she was known as Beatrice.

The giving of human names to birds started in an initiative to help children relate more to them and thereby connect more fully with nature, the environment and conservation issues. Perhaps anyone who feels this is undignified for the wild birds – or, indeed, any animal – might find comfort in T. S. Eliot's theory about the naming of cats: cats have three different names – the name you give them, the name to which they answer and the name that only they know.

Lady had many names. The BBC regularly referred to her as Mabel, but any Internet search reveals that some sites called her Marge. Her several other names included Madge, Lola, Edith, Isla and Maud. On a Lowes blog debate about names a nursery class of three- and four-year-olds chipped in to say that they had named her Jeannie after the osprey in the Hamish McHaggis stories. So, it was cheers to Lady – and all her lovely names – as she sat in her nest with her new chick.

The two unhatched eggs beside them were still part of Mother Nature's plan.

9 *Wings of hope*

The weather changed towards the end of May, with lots of heavy rain – thankfully, because loch and land were drying out. The water level in the loch was low for the time of year and the well on which the Lowes reserve relied was drying. Out on the loch, ducklings were enjoying the rain; black-headed gulls were devouring the black clouds of insects that hovered above its surface. For Lady, though, keeping her brood warm and dry was a full-time job, particularly now there were two.

The chicks were growing fast, as much in a day, relatively, as any human baby might grow in six months. During the first few days after the initial brief immobile stage, they lay quietly in the central bowl until anyone appeared on the nest edge. Then they stood weakly for food, heads wobbling, but quickly collapsed to snuggle together underneath Lady. They were still helpless little balls of downy fluff, vulnerable to the weather and predation.

The wet weather did not last, and the final day of May dawned bright with encouraging news from a few hundred miles further south in England, where the first osprey chick of one reserve's breeding season had hatched at four that morning. Lady's third egg still had not hatched, but although it was running late, there was no cause for concern yet: it would be smaller but not necessarily at a disadvantage. It was normal for osprey chicks to be born up to a week apart, happily to co-exist and go on to fledge, provided there was enough food to go round. If not, Lady would eventually tire of incubating her last egg and either push it out of the nest or to one side, where it would remain, gradually disappearing under fresh bedding and footfall. But her instincts to nurture and protect were so strong that she might continue to incubate for weeks; meanwhile, the egg would be a good pillow for the growing chicks until such time as it got buried or broken, which was what happened.

Lowes had started to wind down its round-the-clock nest protection although other layers of security remained. It was always a relief when the eggs hatched and were no longer a temptation for thieves. The last hurrah was a hatch party to celebrate a job well done and raise a glass to one fine old bird and twenty years of dedicated guarding.

The new nest challenge was Lady's: how to shade her two chicks from the relentless sun in an exposed nest with only a thin limb above it, which offered no natural shade at that time of year. She had her work cut out during the mostly cloudless days that followed, having to stand parasol-like above her chicks for hours on end. But the chicks were daily less vulnerable, and the older one's down was turning dark grey.

By just ten days old osprey nestlings are fairly mobile and begin gallivanting around the nest. By the first week in June, Lady's chicks were waddling around its perimeter, alarmingly close to the edge at times but on much stronger legs. They were especially active whenever a fish was delivered, at which point they would beg as if their lives depended on it – which, of course, they did.

As the days passed, their balance improved, although they still had an hilarious tendency to topple over after a big feed, top heavy from the tiny morsels of fish they would crop in the food storage area of their gullet until they were stuffed to bursting. Fortunately, they had learnt to back up to deposit their droppings over the rim of the nest; some birds eat the faeces of the young during the first few days after hatching as they are rich in partially digested food.

The chicks were exploring ever outwards from the nest bowl, boldly, adventurously, making sense of the nest's barricading depth, which would progressively diminish and flatten out to a platform, as more nest bedding was piled on to freshen things up and provide more horizontal, level space for the growing family. Sometimes exploration went too far. At another Scottish osprey nesting site later that year, a nestling on a recce tipped over the edge. Fortunately, because the nest was being watched, it was seen to be missing, found unharmed on the ground below the nest and put back; it had been a long way down, and the next time it left the nest it would hopefully be on the wing.

Fledging, or flying the nest for the first time, would not happen for five weeks or so. Meanwhile, Lady's chicks were leading a blessed existence. The mostly calm weather at Lowes during their first two weeks was ideal for fishing and Laird had turned into a well-oiled hunting machine, able to satisfy his family's ceaseless demands for food. He had been catching two or three fish a day but had raised his game to five or six, which would just about meet requirements. Lady spent her days serving numerous fish meals – breakfast, elevenses, lunch, afternoon tea, supper, dinner – to a pair of chicks who regularly mobbed her, gaping for food and racing as fast as their wobbly legs could carry them towards her when Laird arrived with a fish.

One day, Laird surprised everyone when he even fed the chicks himself, which male birds never generally do. Later he fed Lady too. He was a wonder, exceeding expectations on all fronts. Fish was so plentiful now that Lady had started stowing it away for later consumption; it was comical to see her brooding her chicks and half a fish.

Full bellies from Laird's regular fish deliveries meant that squabbling over food was rare. Successful nests are known to receive more fish than unsuccessful ones, and well-fed siblings almost never fight; it is only when food is scarce that the persistently hungry chicks, with ever expanding appetites as their bones and feathers are actively growing, and their metabolism reaching its peak, fight over it. Nevertheless, by the end of the first week, sibling rivalry had kicked in, as the chicks established the pecking order. It had to be sorted out early to minimize jockeying for position and endless fights over every mouthful of food, as well as to avoid more serious battles.

Pecking order, which was first observed in hens, is a social hierarchy among birds in which those of higher rank are able to attack or threaten those of lower rank without retaliation. The hen at the bottom of the pecking order has to let everyone else eat first or must rush in to steal and risk being viciously pecked. So it is with ospreys. For an osprey – or, indeed a chicken – it is about finding a place and being clear about territory. They are not ambitious or worried about realizing their potential, about bettering themselves and getting on in life, just determined to survive.

Although the battle among osprey chicks to establish a pecking order looks fierce, real damage is rare, and it is an important stage in the chicks' development that has to be traversed. What happened in Lady's nest that June paled into insignificance when compared with what happens in nests with brood parasites, like cuckoo chicks, emerging from the solitary egg a female cuckoo lays in the nests of other birds.

The cuckoo nestling is born blind, but on hatching it is driven by instinct to eject any other eggs or chicks from the nest so that it rules the roost. It endeavours to get under each egg or chick in turn and roll it on to a hollow in its back, where a patch of sensitive skin triggers the young cuckoo to rear up and cast the egg or chick over the side of the nest. Despite such behaviour, the cuckoo has joined other species, like the grey partridge, house sparrow and turtle dove, on the red list of birds whose populations are in trouble.

Once a pecking order is established on the osprey nest, the dominant chick is always fed first, but the subservient one still gets its share as long as there is no sudden, drastic food shortage, when events can indeed turn nasty. If Laird kept up the good work, that would not happen. A year earlier the outlook had been less rosy.

The May hatching the previous year had taken place in heavy rain, making it hard for the male osprey, Eric, to spot and catch enough fish to feed the family. An unfortunate but predictable feeding pattern set in, whereby the older chick got most of the food, and the younger one grew ever thinner and pitifully weak. The weather got worse, even more difficult for fishing, and the younger chick starved to death because its father was unable to hunt. It was a small tragedy for the birds, with repercussions for their wider resurgence, although a third egg in the clutch did subsequently hatch, five days after the first, and two chicks ultimately fledged. When a population falls to virtual extinction, every life counts.

* * *

It was easy to see how quickly the chicks were growing by comparing their size with the unhatched egg beside them; at the end of their first week both had doubled in size. Their Ferrari-speed growth curve was fuelled by vast quantities of high protein fish. How such tiny birds could consume such enormous amounts of fish, up to six a day between them before too long, was bewildering. Luckily, fish that year was abundant and easy to hunt; only heavy rain, which might cause rivers to spate, and flash flooding would make hunting difficult again for Laird.

The little birds were programmed to eat and needed to gorge themselves to reach their full adult size by the time they were about seven weeks old. Their tight schedule meant they needed to be fledged, fit and as fat as possible for the rigours of autumn migration, some time in late August. It was hard to believe that these osprey nestlings were to leave Scotland for West Africa on their own in about twelve weeks' time.

To the Lowes osprey team's Fiona Hutton, who watched them constantly, the chicks were individually distinct and easy to tell apart. First their colour, then their size helped her to identify them. The year before, the younger of the two remaining chicks had ended up substantially bigger, so she had guessed that was a female. She believed the birds also had different characters, especially according to their sex.

As soon as they learnt to fly, the older one, which Hutton thought was male, was off and rarely seen – more of a masculine trait. The younger, female chick spent more time on the nest, made a lot of noise – as did both chicks, imitating Lady's vocalizations – and copied Lady in moving sticks about or sitting on the egg, which is considered mainly female behaviour. Hutton thought the 2010 season's chicks were probably both females, although the Lowes staff liked to disagree about that. In any case, for a while on the osprey blog the older one became known as Greedy and the younger one as Slim.

Birds use their instinct from the outset, but as they grow they bolster it with experience: they may crouch instinctively in the nest bowl, but they learn about threats from the adult birds. Among the life skills Lady had taught them, by her body language and vocalization, was how to recognize a predator, such as a heron, crow or eagle, and what to do about it. When she put them on alert, the chicks' favoured response was freeze-pose. She was teaching them constantly. Playing dead whenever they sensed anything above them or heard either parent's alarm call presumably was not a technique they enjoyed, but osprey nests are so exposed, offering unguarded youngsters to opportunistic predators virtually on a plate, that it was a good one to instill in them as part of their survival repertoire. They had to endure numerous intruder-bird scares.

One late morning Lady spent a lot of time looking skywards, calling out, disturbed by something above her. According to Rinchen Boardman, one of the permanent staff at Lowes, it was probably just another osprey, either an inquisitive local bird or possibly an unattached juvenile looking to take over the nest, albeit provocatively close. This was not a major nest challenge as earlier in the breeding season, and not a predator buzzard or crow, white-tailed eagle or goshawk that might have posed a real threat to the young birds.

Lady valiantly repelled the intruder with precision shrieking and mantling. Her whistling *kew-kew-kew* grew ever louder to signal rising danger and eventually contracted into a frenzied, furious *chezeek*. Thereafter she extended her wings slightly as a keep-your-distance warning. Later, when the dust had settled, she opened her wings again, fully this time, to shade the chicks. At the end of the day, she was sitting on the nest bathed in evening sunlight, the epitome of calm and contentment, as if nothing in the world would ever worry her again.

One day, unusually, the chicks were alone, playfully sparring, when suddenly they collapsed into the well of the nest and lay there, not moving a single downy feather. Instinctively they knew how best to survive. Their speckled juvenile plumage would later help camouflage them. Juvenile crowns and napes are streaked; the top-side feathers have broad, creamy buff tips, which give them their characteristic barred look (and the eyes remain amber until they are fully adult). When feathers begin to replace down, starting with the rusty-gold pin, or pen, feathers on the head and neck, the chicks sport a curious combination of both. Pin feathers are immature and develop before the vanes, the flat part on either side of the shaft, appear. The darker body, or contour, feathers emerge a little later; finally, the outer feathers of the wing and tail, known as the primary large or secondary small flight feathers, and rectrices, or tail flight feathers, appear, at about three to four weeks old.

The chicks would have their first full set when they were about six weeks old. Young ospreys, like other young birds of prey, tend to have wing and tail feathers that are longer than the adults'. This is to give them more lift and provide a helpful boost in flight to compensate for their lack of experience. They spend a lot of their time preening their feathers with their bill, cleaning off the down and waxy feather casings. Preening is a job for life, not just about oiling the feathers but also rearranging them and locking the barbs as well as removing lice, the pests that feed on feather protein.

Taking care of their plumage would be key to the chicks' survival. Feathers are unique to birds. They evolved from reptilian scales, and birds still possess scales on the lower parts of their legs and feet. The number of feathers they have varies; one bird said to have a great many is the whistling or tundra swan, which spends time in the wastes of Arctic North America, an environment with underlying permafrost; it winters in the western and coastal eastern regions of the USA. It can have as many as twenty-five thousand feathers during winter and undoubtedly needs them to keep warm. It is also said that large birds, like the raptors, which include the osprey, may have just as many.

Once grown, feathers seal off at the base so a fully developed feather is effectively dead, just like the human fingernail, although the muscles attached to the base of each feather can move individual feathers to help keep them in place. Feathers are made from the same fibrous protein, keratin, as fingernails (as are hair, horn and skin, not forgetting birds' bills and talons). Without feathers, with the protection and insulation they provide and the many other different jobs that the various types do, birds are helpless.

Feathers have assumed human importance too, symbolic of ascension, spirituality, divinity. To the Native American chiefs who wear them they signify celestial wisdom and spirit communication. When, in 2009, US President Barack Obama promised to end his country's two-century neglect of its Native American tribes, he addressed representatives from more than four hundred – several of whom wore elaborate feather headdresses.

Eagle feathers, in particular, are esteemed because they come from the most powerful birds of prey, which soar and glide on air currents high above land, an activity that is considered to endow them with a higher perspective on life below. An eagle's feather is symbolic of rank and status in a variety of cultures, from Highland clan chiefs, with the three eagle feathers in their bonnets, to the Native Americans with their headdresses.

In Ancient Egyptian religion, Maat, the personification of truth, justice and cosmic order, was said to weigh the heart of someone newly deceased on a scale balanced with a feather – her symbol, seen on her head – to determine their soul's worth. In the UK, the heraldic badge of the Prince of Wales includes feathers, three silver (or white) ones that rise through a gold coronet of alternate crosses and fleur-de-lis. It was first adopted as a crest by the eldest son of Edward, Prince of Wales (the Black Prince), in the fourteenth century; three white feathers are now also the symbol of the Welsh Rugby Union. A similar three-feathers symbol is often used as a seal in signet rings, used to authenticate official documents.

It was early summer, and the days were becoming ever longer at Lowes, with the western sky still pale even as late as eleven at night; the extended daylight hours meant the birds were active for longer, and herein lay one of the secrets of the osprey's choice of Scotland as one of its preferred breeding grounds: the extra day-time hunting hours were vital when the chicks were at their hungriest. When they had acquired their first complete set of plumage, about early July, they would no longer be chicks but juveniles, and look more like adult birds, except for their speckled backs and wings.

For now, they were becoming more vocal; the eldest seemed to be imitating its mother's encouragement call – *quee-quee-quee* – to Laird, still fishing for Scotland. At three weeks old, around 12 June, they were better able to stand for more than a few wobbly seconds. They looked endearingly comical, especially their supersize floppy feet, which were growing faster than their heads (initially the biggest part of them). Of course this was as it should be, because an osprey's feet are its working parts on which its future survival depends. Although the bill is as sharp and lethal as it looks, it is the feet that catch and dispatch the fish. A glance at Lady's, especially the enormous size and strength of her talons, confirmed this.

After about five weeks there would be no more fooling around, however clownish their feet, as they began to learn to stand on a fish, to anchor it as they pulled and twisted it apart with their beak. It is vital for the young birds to learn to shred their own food rather than having it ripped for them by their mother. As a further sign of their impending independence, their father was bringing in less food: fish deliveries level off when the chicks are about a month old, a couple of weeks before they fledge, to give them some incentive to leave and encourage their independence.

It seemed odd that the chicks' well-developed feet and legs took so long to support ever-growing bodies for more than a few wobbly seconds. Of course, balance is an aspect of development that works in tandem with the extension of the wings. And they had begun to stretch them more frequently, although fledging was not anticipated until the second week of July. Plenty of practice flapping could be expected, though. The chicks would increasingly tour the nest but sometimes rise up and stretch out their wings, holding on tight with their talons, strengthening their muscles prior to little leaps. The confines of the nest made it impractical for the pair to do this at the same time – if they did, chaos ensued.

From early July, when they were about seven weeks old, they would do vertical lift-offs, just a few inches above the nest at first, wings beating, then increase, warily, to a few feet, collapsing back each time into the welcome safety of the nest. Warm, gusty breezes were ideal practice conditions pre-fledging. Male birds generally fledge first because they are smaller and lighter than the females. After their first flight, of only a few minutes, they become more adventurous, exploring the neighbourhood around the nest site, although they remain alert for food deliveries and return at any sniff of a fish. They practise flying freely for a few weeks after fledging in preparation for their mighty migration. About three weeks after their first flight, they start to soar high on fixed wings, using the thermals, but most of an osprey's flight involves beating its wings constantly or hovering above potential prey, much like an outsize kestrel. Landing was a skill to be learnt, too, sometimes with hilarious results; much like take-off, it often took a while to perfect.

A great deal of new wildlife was to be found out and about on the reserve, enjoying its first summer. One day in early June there was a red squirrel at the osprey's nest, and two baby squirrels, or kits, were later spotted (their drey was thought to be in the same tree). In the waters of the loch, far below, a roe deer could be seen swimming, with Canada goslings and mallard ducklings to keep it company.

Great crested grebe young were also in evidence. Summer downpours had flooded the grebe nests in previous years and washed away the eggs; they had enjoyed the loch's first successful hatchings in three years. On land common lizards, slow worms, weasels and stoats were spotted, and butterflies provided the finishing touches to an altogether joyful scene with their animated fluttering. One off-key note was struck amid the burgeoning evidence of life: none of the five blue tit chicks on the reserve's televised nest had fledged.

However, all of this activity pointed to a successful breeding season at Lowes. At the visitor centre, Peter Ferns and his team were aware that Lady's chicks would soon be ready for their rings. Bird ringing, attaching individually marked rings to the legs of wild birds, is vital to conservation field research because it helps to identify a bird and chart its lifetime progress, enabling a more scientific, targeted approach to conservation of bird populations and their habitats. The National Bird Ringing Programme is coordinated by the British Trust for Ornithology (BTO), with its network of some 2,500 highly trained and licensed volunteers, who, by 2010, were ringing more than 900,000 birds every year. Just one in fifty birds ringed is subsequently found, so every report of a ringed bird is significant.

In late June and July, many young ospreys are ringed, and it was hoped that Lady's two chicks would be among them that year. By the time the chicks were between five and seven weeks old, a couple of weeks after the last week of June, Lowes planned not just to ring them but also to fit them with satellite-transmitter tags. It had to be done after the adult ospreys had fully bonded with their chicks, at about five weeks, so they would not abandon them, but before the chicks were able to fly or bold enough to leap out of the nest with potentially fatal consequences. This window of opportunity was fast approaching. Soon the Lowes team would have the chance to solve the mystery of the birds' migratory journeys.

Ringing and tagging was a skilled job done under special licence by a team of expert tree climbers, bird ringers and vets. It would happen either in the nest, with Lady circling furiously above, or on the ground, after the trained team had lowered the chicks in a small sack. The birds' welfare and safety was of prime concern throughout, and each chick would undergo a full health-and-strength check in advance of any ringing or tagging.

If all was well, each bird would be ringed with a BTO lightweight metal ring and a coloured plastic one on the other leg. Each satellite tag, which weighed about an ounce, around 1.5 per cent of the chick's bodyweight, was attached to a harness that was fitted to the bird like a tiny rucksack. The tags lasted for three years, as long as the battery was sufficiently charged with sunlight via its miniature solar panel. Tagging was a safe and proven research method that caused no harm to the birds. Neither tags nor rings affected their behaviour. Crucially, they did not cause navigation errors, which would have disqualified them as a research tool.

The tags would transmit information about the birds' journey via the Global Positioning System (GPS) to the Lowes computer system, sending hourly updates on geographical position, accurate to within sixty-five feet, as well as the bird's direction, height of flight and prevailing flight conditions. The purpose of tagging was not just idle curiosity. It had the potential to unlock secrets about the young ospreys' behaviour, to build up a detailed picture of each bird's migration route, which would aid conservationists in helping the birds (or, at least, provide the necessary know-how on how best not to hamper them).

Satellite tagging enabled conservationists to learn and understand a great deal more about what ospreys did on their migration, an instinctive process determined by their hereditary programming. The details of the young birds' first migration would be revealed, as would the reason for an older osprey's failure to return – as with Lady's mate of fourteen years – and any pattern to failed migrations. Lady had attracted another mate, but what had happened to Eric?

No one knew precisely the preferred places, the stopping points, usually wetlands and estuaries, where the birds liked to land and feed. By discovering this kind of detail, it was at least possible that governments might be encouraged to work together internationally to protect the birds. It was known, for example, that many UK ospreys like Lady passed through a big estuary system on the coasts of Spain and Portugal, which was now a protected site for the birds. There were equivalents in Mauritania, Morocco, Senegal and elsewhere that could be flagged up as potential conservation sites.

Tagging is not yet widespread, but even with only a tiny proportion of the osprey population tagged, it has given intriguing little snippets of information, and conservationists are keen to know more.

One of the drawbacks to satellite tagging is its high price: each transmitter costs a few thousand pounds. It was to raise the money to pay for them that amateur cyclist and Lowes volunteer Toby Green decided to undertake a sponsored cycle ride from Land's End to John O'Groats. It was a completely mad notion, but he did a great job and raised a lot of money through sponsorship. One Saturday in early May, he set off on his own incredible journey, with no support team and all his equipment, including a tent, packed on his bike.

It was a tough call, although nothing, he was gracious enough to admit, compared to the hardships of the annual osprey migration. By the end of his ride, Green was even more in awe of the osprey's amazing endurance, and the money he raised gave Lowes the wherewithal to engage in some important and fascinating scientific research on its ospreys, starting with Lady's new chicks. It was a prospect that filled the osprey team at Lowes with hope, a potentially brand-new phase for them and their ospreys.

Summer had started in earnest, and the chicks were growing and edging ever nearer the point at which they could be ringed and tagged; soon they would fledge and venture into the wider world; soon Lady and her chicks would directly assist conservationists in furthering the osprey's resurgence and helping future generations of the species to thrive. It was all looking wonderfully promising – until the third week in June, when life at Lowes went from day to night in the beat of a wing.

10 Back from the brink

Whatever ailed Lady weakened her so much that she remained motionless on the floor of the nest, hardly opening her eyes. She was virtually comatose, with barely enough strength to move; her breathing was erratic. She acted at times as if she were a new mother and seemed confused at what to do with a fish that Laird had delivered to the nest. Her month-old chicks, huddled together beside her, looked pitiful. That weekend marked the start of a journey that quickly headed into uncharted territory.

At around eight the previous evening, Lady had fed her chicks after a fish drop from Laird. Fiona Hutton, about to leave for the night, noted Laird's record delivery of ten, later eleven, fish that day. Consequently, two happy, well-fed chicks snuggled beneath their mother, who subsequently fed herself. Later, in the golden light of the setting sun, Lady had sat perched on the edge of the nest, flapping her wings a little, before briefly flying off. Peace and quiet had reigned as she returned to the nest shortly thereafter; night closed in.

The first signs that all was not well came just before five on Saturday morning when Laird delivered his first fish of the day, which Lady ignored. As he flew off, taking his catch with him, Lady looked up briefly, then bowed her head again. The chicks were clearly hungry, cheeping their protest. Eventually, it was obvious that Lady was unable to stand or fold her wings. It was highly unusual for her to lie prostrate in the nest during daylight hours.

Shortly after seven, one of the chicks attempted to tuck itself underneath its mother. Lady struggled to stand and cover it with a wing but instead fell back into the bottom of the nest. Just after nine, she raised herself again briefly but unsteadily on her legs and, keeping her wings spread for balance, wobbled at the nest edge. Minutes later she lay down again in the nest bowl, one wing sheltering her chicks, her head dropped. Laird arrived with supplies, voiced his alarm, increasingly loud and urgent, then left with yet another uneaten fish. The chicks emerged from under their mother and started to shuffle around in the nest above her. It began to rain.

Lowes' assembled team of expert ornithologists and veterinary specialists predicted the worst. At one point they reviewed the nest-webcam footage from the Friday night onwards but found no marks on Lady to suggest she might be injured. All anyone could come up with was that perhaps her illness was age-related; after all, everyone gets old and dies. Whatever was wrong, it was distressing to watch Lady suffer. It was the extraordinary speed at which she had gone downhill that was hard to understand; she was failing so fast and unexpectedly. Perthshire ranger Emma Rawling's background in veterinary nursing and animal welfare gave her a fairly good insight into wild birds' health. In her experience wild animals would generally hide illness as long as they could. They would not want to show any sign of weakness that might make them easy prey. It was Darwinian survival of the fittest; Lady was a tough old bird, a true survivor – until now.

The bottom line was that specialist avian vets and people with experience of ospreys in captivity were available to help, but any wild animal is hard to treat medically. Ospreys are notoriously bad patients. They are not used to being handled by humans, or being around human smells, so they usually die of the stress it causes them. This was a consideration very much in everyone's mind: attempting to help Lady risked doing her more harm than good. In the short term, it might have made everyone feel better to do something, anything, but if it were to her ultimate detriment, it would have been wrong.

That Saturday morning debate had raged at Lowes before the decision was made to leave her alone. As a wildlife reserve, Lowes' conservation policy was non-interference in the natural life of wild animals and letting nature take its course. That did not mean anyone directly involved was immune to the distressing turn of events: staff and public alike, who were watching the nest webcam at Lowes, were regularly in tears over the next few days.

From Finland to Canada, Oman, Australia, the US, Japan, Peru and twenty other countries, world attention became focused on Lady and her chicks as the weekend progressed. The Lowes team was moved by this concern and interest in their osprey and felt public pressure to do something, which was compounded by the personal pressure they were under. It was a heart-wrenching struggle, a tug of love. At gut level, they wanted to help their dying bird, 'our bird', as Lowes often called Lady, yet all the while they believed nature must do things its way – and that some things are best left undone.

Any involvement with wildlife raises the dilemma of when to help and when to stand back. Peter Ferns shared the public frustration and sadness. He had spent many a night with Lady, watching her incubate eggs, sometimes in atrocious weather. During his first year doing nights on osprey watch, the temperature had dropped to −7°C, and snow had fallen heavily, completely covering her. She had been a fighter then and was proving to be so now in what he knew could be his last days with her. His hope, however, was that her suffering would not be prolonged, as he made clear when he said: 'This is nature, she's a wild bird and if she's coming to the end of her time I think it would be better if we just left her to it. She's been a fantastic bird.'

Emma Rawling had not been working at the reserve for

nearly as long as Peter Ferns or some of the others involved, but she still felt a strong emotional bond. After all, she had been watching Lady every day and sometimes throughout the night since the osprey's return at the end of March. She could not remember the number of times she had done the midnight-to-eight-o'clock shift and watched every nuance of Lady's life. She felt that she had got to know her. She felt an intense emotional pull to do something, but as a scientist she stood firm: she would do only what was best for the bird.

But it was not just about Lady: there were her chicks to consider, still dependent on her for food and protection – although on the latter they were not so vulnerable now that they were three-quarters full size. By midday on the Saturday, Laird had visited the nest a few times with fish, but without Lady to shred and serve it, he was bewildered by what to do with it. The chicks had eaten a great deal of fish in the previous twenty-four hours, so, with food stored in their crops, they would be fine for a while.

However, they were still continuously ravenous, and, of course, if they did not feed eventually, they would starve to death. Fortunately, it was quite warm that day, despite a cool breeze. After much debate, their fate was decided: if the chicks showed signs of neglect, of being left alone and undernourished, then the Lowes osprey team would consider providing fish to the nest via a climber, at least initially to see if the young birds could deal with that arrangement. Any notion of captivity was out of the question.

A chink of light appeared in the early afternoon as the chicks pecked ineffectually at a perch Laird had deposited on the nest. He watched their pathetic attempts to feed themselves, and finally, mercifully, took over, shredding it and serving them himself. This small victory in the war of attrition that Lady's illness had become saw the chicks' chances of survival rise and made Laird hero of the hour. But, in the perpetual seesaw of emotion that weekend, joy was soon tempered by sorrow as Lady, unable even to lift her head, continued to refuse offers of fish from Laird. Her eyes remained closed and she had lost the strength in her legs and wings. It was increasingly clear that her life was slipping away. Now she was aware that her chicks were being cared for, perhaps she would let go peacefully.

Throughout the long night that followed, the wind blew around the nest; the faint calls of the chicks could be heard as they got up to move around or tried to nestle under Lady's wing and shelter from the cool night air, even though their feathers were now adequate protection against the coldest of June nights. Lady was still moving occasionally, and looked as if she would survive the night. Laird was most likely roosting in a nearby Scots pine and would be back at the nest site well before the sun rose above the horizon. There was talk of an otter having been seen on the south shore of the loch, the first sighting in a while. Otters are semi-aquatic animals, and it was presumably living in a holt at the water's edge.

149

Light showed in the sky at just before three on the Sunday morning, and the dawn chorus was in full swing. It was time for the oyster-catchers to let everyone know they were ready for the day. The chilling bark of a fox had been heard beneath the osprey nest as Lowes kept watch over Lady, who was still struggling on, although her breathing had become shallow and laboured. It was clear that she was suffering; it was hoped that it would not be long now before she died.

By Monday, everyone agreed that Lady had less than forty-eight hours to live. She had stopped eating and with no liquid intake either she was starting to look sunken; her co-ordination was poor. A bird of her size could last only four days without water, which gave her until Tuesday evening. Meanwhile, the team planned to remove her from the nest if she died. The chicks would react to human presence as they would to any potential predator and collapse flat in the nest, not moving in their pretence at invisibility. Fortunately, they were still too young to try to leave the nest.

At first light on Monday, as the sun stood still on the longest day of the year, an enduring radiance enveloped the loch, creating a luminosity that was eerie yet calming. Lady was still hanging on. The previous two days had been a bumpy ride, but as the tawny owls called and the loch gently lapped the shore, it was clear that life was carrying on at Lowes. Two squirrel kits chased one another up and down, round and round a tree. Black-and-white striped great crested grebe chicks once again hitched a ride across the loch on their mother's back. A blackbird was singing tunefully, perhaps simply because it could. And one woodpecker continued to feed her young even though her chick was quite big enough to feed itself.

Against all that vibrant life, Lady quietly battled on. Her plight had hit the nation's headlines and featured on the television news; she was living out her final days in the public eye, as nearly a quarter of a million viewers followed live footage of her.

Later that night many also saw her rally: the world watched in amazement as one sick osprey, thought to have only hours to live, did a three-point turn on the head of a pin. Two film production teams had been at Lowes in late June for some pre-planned filming: the first had chanced to see Lady sink into the rapid decline that led to reports of her imminent death; the second was privileged to watch her miraculous reprieve, snatched from the jaws of death by some guardian angel. What a blessed bird; Lady luck indeed.

Emma Rawling had been among those who were astonished to see Lady pull back from the brink and watch as she left the nest for the first time in several days – coincidentally, when the second BBC production crew had been filming at Lowes. Lady had first shown signs of recovery when she stood on shaky legs, then walked, ever more wobbly, to the edge of the nest. From the nest, she took off, at first dipping sharply, struggling, as if she were about to crash-land or belly-flop on the water. Ever resilient, she managed to land on the other side of the bay, on the ground, something ospreys rarely did, preferring to perch above it, where they are less vulnerable to predators. In any case, they have no need to land on lakesides or river banks to drink as they get almost all their moisture from their diet, at most scooping a gulp of water as they fly over it.

At the water's edge, Lady drank several long draughts of water – it was clear from how sunken she looked that she was severely dehydrated – then washed. She was caked in her own faeces, an unusual state for ospreys because they are such fastidiously clean birds – on the nest, they defecate over the edge to keep it fresh. She had been lying in her own filth for days; her lochside bath was a strip-wash, which was all she could manage, the spirit-raising attempt of one so recently returned from death's door. But however token the effort, it would have depleted the diminished energy reserves of a mother bird, with two demanding young chicks, who had lain half dead in the nest beside her for more than three days. Lady was one very sick bird who was not going to give in without a fight.

After Lady had been at the loch's edge for about half an hour, panic rose in the watchers. What if she stayed sitting there? What if she could not get back to the nest? On the ground she was vulnerable, never more so than in her weakened state. But Lady did leave the lochside, taking off slowly, quite unlike her normal strong, direct flight. During the four or five times that she circled the nest site it became increasingly clear that she was disoriented and having difficulty locating the nest. Eventually, poignantly, it was her chicks who helped her: their cries drew her back.

The relief and joy felt by Lady's legions of followers at her return to the nest was immense. For days they had watched her suffer, fearing the worst, and when she finally rose from her sick bed, there had been great rejoicing. But when she had almost failed at that final hurdle, as if at the crossroads of life and death, it had been almost too much to bear. She had chosen the path leading back to life and her chicks had guided her home. She had returned to where she belonged, to her nest and her babies, to the hearts of those who loved her.

This was the turning point, after which Lady started back on the road to recovery. She began eating again, then resumed serving the chicks. Over the following days, she fed more, just little bits to start, and began to leave the nest again, taking short flights. She could be seen sitting up straight, on her favourite perch, the long, sky-reaching branch to the left of the nest that she liked. She was preening again too and doing all the normal things that encouraged everyone in the belief that she might have made it through her long, dark night. Yet the fear never ebbed away entirely that her miraculous recovery might in the end prove a false dawn.

One thing was unambiguous: Laird had turned out to be an ideal partner and a dedicated father; a star in the Lowes firmament. No one could have asked for better – not just in terms of his parenting prowess and the amount of fishing he had done, fetching regular food supplies for his family, but also in the fantastic dedication he had shown when faced with a challenge. He had succeeded with flying colours. A few people at least might have dared to think that if Lady did not return the following year, or the one after that, this male osprey, Lady's new mate, was now a proven breeder and closely bonded with the Lowes site; he would definitely come back to it, nature permitting, and continue the line. One day, eventually, as part of life's inevitable circle, he would find another female and continue; that day would mark the start of a hopefully long association with Laird and a new era for the osprey at Lowes.

But, such thoughts, although natural, were a tad premature because Lady was still very much alive, growing stronger by the day. For Emma Rawling, this was itself a miracle. During her extensive experience of rescue work with raptors, she had never seen a bird so ill pull through. Lady had gone beyond the point of no return and, to everyone's astonishment, she had made it back. To the great relief of one and all, nature had found the best possible resolution.

It was three-thirty a.m., just before dawn on the day after midsummer, and the birds were singing to announce what looked set to be a magnificent sunrise. Lady was sitting quietly in one side of the nest but had been restless throughout the dark hours; her eyes were still sunken and would remain like that until she had taken enough fluids for her body to fill out again. It was a good morning to fish, which was just as well as the chicks had been calling for food since before it had got light.

The following day, Peter Ferns's post on the osprey blog was positive: 'What a great sight to come in to this morning, our Lady feeding the chicks. She is getting stronger and stronger all the time, and we are more hopeful than we have been for her survival.' But, he cautioned, whatever had just happened to her might have a lasting effect on her. For the moment it was best to enjoy each day as it came.

After Lady had eaten her first fish in several days, the Scottish Wildlife Trust put out an announcement thanking everyone for their interest in their fundraising campaign to raise money to satellite-track their juvenile osprey chicks. It had made enquiries about getting the satellite tracking done that year, although it appeared unlikely given the short timescale. But the recent news about Lady meant they would definitely not be tracking or ringing any chicks that year. Everyone, not least the osprey, had seen quite enough drama for one season, and any interference to the nest at that crucial stage might jeopardize Lady's hoped-for recovery. All being well, next year's Lowes brood would be satellite-tagged. The Trust had been amazed and grateful for support from all corners of the globe at such a stressful time; staff at the reserve were excited at her progress, describing her as a phenomenal bird.

* * *

A soft rain fell at Lowes on 1 July, lightly rippling the surface of the loch and making music in the woods as the water dripped from the trees. It was welcome but set a precedent for some fairly gloomy summer weather that month, which turned out to be the wettest and coolest period so far of that year's breeding season. That day the chicks snuggled together in the nest against the rain, testing out their new waterproof feathers, not as effective as those of a diving duck, but impermeable enough. Lady, no longer required as their umbrella, sat high above them, looking regal on her perch. As the life-and-death drama had gone on around the chicks, they had carried on regardless, once their food supply had been re-established.

As anticipated, by early July the chicks were really starting to flap their wings, strengthening vital flight muscles before their expected first sortie in a week or so. Their enormous feet seemed more coordinated, and they had begun to use their talons, too, instead of just balancing on their heels. Their head waggle, the side-to-side movement ospreys use when fishing or trying to focus on something, was a new development. And it was noticeable that their eyesight was developing as fast as everything else: they practised homing in on whatever caught their attention out on the loch. When it comes to hunting, the eyes have it for the osprey: their vision is acute, unlike that of some birds, such as the barn owl, which relies more on its sharp hearing to hunt by day and night. It can hunt with deadly accuracy in complete darkness, guided only by its ears. When it came to birds' ears generally – other than ostriches' – they are little different from those of reptiles or amphibians. Most, like the osprey, show no outward sign of an ear, unless their feathers are parted.

One gusty, breezy day, the chicks' thoughts turned to flight. It was the perfect weather for it, and Lady had been spending much more of her time off the nest, as encouragement to her chicks to follow her. There had been a surprise one morning when one of the chicks had taken advantage of an especially strong gust of wind and flapped robustly several feet above the nest. Once they fledged and until their migration, they would continue to return to the nest to receive food deliveries from Laird, who would bring in whole live fish and leave the chicks to practise feeding themselves.

They might have a go at fishing, mostly taking odd runs at the water, not seriously trying to catch anything – although they might if they were lucky – but learning to judge distances, angles and speeds for successful future hunting strikes. By the end of the first week of July both chicks were able largely to feed themselves. Their ever-strengthening feet were better able to stand on the fish so that they could tear at it with their beaks. They were also incredibly vocal – it was one of the noisiest times of the year on the nest.

On the morning of 11 July, the older chick spread its wings, hovered above the nest and took its maiden flight, flying freely into a fresh breeze. Lady had flown back to her perch, presumably to act as a landing beacon, although the chick had to try a few times, due to inexperience in a strong wind, before it returned safely. The following day chick number two felt the wind beneath its wings, despite ferocious thunderstorms. Training flights, circling the loch, ensued and, with their wing muscles getting used to all the new demands and in need of conditioning, they would often perch somewhere nearby to rest and build the energy to fly back to the nest.

By mid-July the continuing bad weather made fishing difficult for the adult ospreys, with poor visibility and sizeable waves on the loch. All the wild birds had begun using the more sheltered bays on the loch's leeward side for foraging and roosting. Ospreys, young and old, started sitting in the sheltered trees across from the nest. Wherever they roosted, however, the chicks were never too far from the nest, always within easy reach of fish deliveries.

The end of the third week in July brought sunshine at last. As the sun warmed up, the steam started rising from the woods, and all Lowes' wildlife were drying out. It was a truly glorious time with the whole world seemingly fresh-washed and plump with moisture. Lady was no exception, preening proudly on her nest perch, no doubt enjoying the sun on her feathers. Perhaps it made her dream of Africa with its balmy winds, hot nights, bounteous fish. A few days earlier, unusually, all four ospreys had sat briefly together on the nest again. It was unlikely to happen for much longer.

As the end of July approached, Lady was spending less and less time on the nest, and frequenting less often her favourite viewing perch atop it, which overlooked the bay. The juvies, as the chicks were now sometimes called, had a long bath one day and still occasionally lay flat in the nest as if they had forgotten how to perch. Often, though, they soared ever higher and further from the loch for longer and longer periods. Laird continued to stop by briefly to drop fish into the nest, but was soon gone.

The amount of intruder activity around the nest increased from mid-July, which was not surprising, given that other young ospreys in nearby nests were also fledging, and the adult birds were frantic with the effort of satisfying food demands. The ospreys' alarm calls, which could be heard everywhere, were more token protest at neighbours who were getting too close than anything more serious. It was hard to believe, watching Lady, busy chasing across the loch after yet another intruder, that she had ever been ill. She was flying strongly, which augured well for her long journey south. But when would that be?

Lady usually left early on migration, as the adult females do, often at the start of August, but this year was different. She might need to postpone her migration to build up her strength, or she might not migrate at all.

On 5 August, however, as more than two thousand wildlife enthusiasts watched live online for Lady to return to her nest, the realization slowly dawned that she had left. She had not been seen at the loch since the previous morning, although someone claimed later that day to have seen her flying over the woods. When, at the end of a long day's waiting, she did not appear, the indications were that she had taken to the skies to begin her annual migration to West Africa.

The following day, when she had still not come back, Lowes confirmed that their magnificent Lady had indeed left them for the year. She had flown off right on schedule, her timing entirely consistent with her average departure dates over the preceding decades. That was Lady, a redoubtable, reliable force of nature.

It was normal and natural that she should head south at that time of year: like all the birds, her instinct to migrate was overwhelmingly strong. But the journey she faced was fraught with danger, and concerns mounted that this could be her last migration. Her journey would probably take her over England, although some birds head west over Ireland. Then she would most likely fly over western France, Spain or Portugal and ever onwards to West Africa.

En route she would rely on a continual chain of rivers, wetlands and estuaries for food and shelter or face starvation and utter exhaustion. Perhaps she would encounter bad weather, especially gale-force Atlantic winds, which could blow her out to sea where she would not survive long, or perilous desert dust and sandstorms. She risked random shooting, too, near the Mediterranean especially, and possibly lethal power-line or rubbish entanglements.

If she survived that journey, she could look forward to

about five months in her traditional wintering grounds, building herself up again with some much-needed rest and recuperation before she faced north once more for a repeat run back to Lowes in the spring.

The signs that Lady would migrate successfully that autumn were encouraging: she had beaten the odds and made a good recovery from whatever had ailed her. She had fed herself up throughout July and increased her body-weight before her journey, so it was likely that she would be strong enough to endure its rigours. Her departure was met with good wishes, the hope that her strength would last, her luck would hold and her journey would be safe. There was great admiration for her, and all the birds that made these extraordinary journeys every year. But there was apprehension about her departure, too, a heavy, lingering sadness at her leaving, with accompanying doubts about whether or not she would be seen again at Lowes. Experts were quoted as giving her a 50 per cent chance of return the following year.

Her departure sparked a flood of farewells from around the world. Peter Ferns found it especially moving to know that Lady had left Loch of the Lowes: he knew he might not see her again. Of course he had always understood that one day she would not return, would never be seen again in Scottish skies, never patiently, diligently, industriously, with her mate, rebuild the nest for that year's brood, lovingly raise chicks on that vast and sprawling latticework of hard-wearing sticks interlined with soft, spongy mosses atop the tall Scots pine, make her slow, whistling, haunting *kew-kew-kew* guard calls across the loch or sit stock still but alert on her perching branch high above the water. The spell that Lady cast over Lowes would one day be broken.

But for now, that season, with Lady gone, Lowes had about two weeks left in which to watch over its ospreys. As August progressed, Laird's thoughts turned to leaving, which he did some time towards the end of the month. The chicks spent less and less time on the nest from the middle of August, then they, too, slipped away.

Because ospreys migrate individually, they had needed to be fully independent of their parents before they began their southward journey. Learning to fish for themselves was part of that. Just how they learn to fish after fledging is a mystery, in which genetic instinct perhaps plays a key role, although the male bird may do some demonstrating. The general belief is that the chicks do not fish for themselves until both parents have left for the south, but Lowes had photographed chicks doing just that. Whatever the truth, hunting was a tough call, with its goal of a small, moving underwater target that required a simultaneous dive to catch it. Unsurprisingly, young ospreys of up to six months old are said to be half as successful as adults at hunting, making their hunts longer and more arduous.

What is not in doubt is the amazingly fast and demanding growth curve these birds undergo, and just how big a challenge they face in their first weeks and months alone.

The fact that they were able to make the journey, on their own, to West Africa was extraordinary. At the human equivalent of ten years old, they would get there without parent bird or sibling, map or compass, catching their dinner with their feet on the way. Of course, they had their own inbuilt GPS, probably some combination of visual clues – it is known they fly more in good clear weather – and genetic instinct, along with some form of geomagnetic perception not yet understood. But it remains an astonishing, hazardous feat, part of the magic of ospreys.

Most ospreys take between a month and six weeks to make the journey in autumn to their wintering sites but are considerably faster on the way up in spring, when the breeding instinct is strong and they must get to the nest first. Females make more stopovers than males (hence the earlier departure). Young birds tend to make more stops, too, and wander more before settling down into an habitual yearly pattern; it could take them up to eight weeks to make their first full migration.

The birds would fly predominantly during the day, but sometimes at night, particularly over large stretches of water, at considerable heights, up to a hundred or so miles a day and even fly for up to forty-eight hours or more without stopping. Lady's chicks would likely spend the first three to five years in their wintering grounds until they were sexually mature, then return to the UK to breed. They would head in the direction of their nest site, finding their own sites and partners on the way, ready to continue their mother's legacy. It was heartening to think that some of Lady's descendants were out there helping repopulate new areas.

By the end of August, all of the Lowes ospreys had gone, adding to the foretaste of autumn that the already cold and misty mornings, the absence of swifts and their screeching cries over nearby Dunkeld provided. The time of mellow fruitfulness was approaching, and the autumn would bring huge movements of migrating birds to Lowes – some, like Lady, heading south to a warmer climate, others seeking refuge in the UK from the Arctic winter. Vast flocks of birds would assemble at Lowes to feed or, at twilight, fly in to form large roosts to keep warm, such as the hundreds of starlings seen diving and swirling in a tight formation, framed against a November sunset of fiery orange and dusky pink. But that summer's end found Lowes suffering from empty-nest syndrome, following the departure of all their ospreys on autumn migration. The occasional ospreys that were still seen nearby were mostly passing through on their way south, using the loch as a good place to stop for supper.

The last day of August brought good news of an osprey chick born several seasons previously, in 2001, at Lowes. She had been sighted in Dumfries and Galloway and was one of Lady's daughters. Whatever Lady's fate that winter, at the end of a tumultuous year, her legacy lived on.

Some things you might not know about ospreys

1. Osprey is the common name for *Pandion haliaetus*. The word 'osprey' comes from the Old French *ospres*, derived from the Latin *ossifragus*, meaning 'bone breaking'. The osprey, with its worldwide range, is commonly known in numerous languages, including Cornish, Gaelic, Galician, Japanese and Vietnamese. There are multiple names for the osprey in certain languages, such as Welsh, Spanish and Portuguese. Sadly, there are no longer any breeding ospreys in Portugal, despite its many names.

2. Pandionidae is the osprey family name. It is the only species in this family. There were several prehistoric species of osprey, all of which have been described from fossils. Fossils of the osprey have been found on the

island of Tonga, where it was probably exterminated by arriving humans.

3. Osprey *Pandion haliaetus* has four subspecies: *Pandion haliaetus carolinensis*, found in North America; *Pandion haliaetus cristatus*, found in Australasia; *Pandion haliaetus haliaetus*, found in Eurasia; and *Pandion haliaetus ridgwayi*, found in the Caribbean. The Australasian osprey is the smallest subspecies.

4. The osprey is among a list of birds in the Bible, in the Old Testament Book of Leviticus (11:13–19), deemed 'an abomination', meaning that it is taboo and not to be eaten. Other birds on the list, which varies according to translation, include the eagle, the kite, the owl, the cuckoo, the cormorant, the swan and the lapwing. There is a school of thought that claims this designation is meant to indicate not that the birds are disgusting but that it is against nature to harm them, that they are sacred.

5. The osprey first appeared in literature in *The Birds*, a play written by Aristophanes in about 410 BC, in which two Athenians seek a Utopian refuge from maddening city life by founding a city of birds, located between Earth and Olympus. The idealism of their new city – named 'Cloud Cuckoo Land' – becomes corrupted; its decline and fall are portrayed by one man (the chorus) as twenty-four different species of bird.

6. The missionary tale of a Bolivian Indian inserting the bone of an osprey under the skin of his arm, in the hope of absorbing its hunting prowess, has become engrained in osprey lore.

7. According to Robin Hull's *Scottish Birds: Culture and Tradition*, it was believed, as late as the sixteenth century, that only one osprey foot was armed with talons for fishing while the other was used purely for swimming.

8. In 1981 there were seventeen US states with no breeding ospreys; by 2007 there were just four. According to Alan Poole, in some parts of North America, ospreys readily nest among people – near houses, bustling highways and harbours.

9. In parts of Mexico, where trees are scarce, ospreys often nest on tall cacti. In the Caribbean (coastal Belize), most nests are found in flat-topped mangroves.

10. During an egg raid from RSPB Loch Garten, thieves daubed two chicken eggs with boot polish to deceive their pursuers and tried to conceal the real osprey eggs until the heat had died down. In 1964, eggers even attempted to cut down the nest tree. The Loch Garten ospreys may take the crown as the most studied birds in the world, with complete progress records for every year of the past half-century.

11. In some parts of the world, osprey eggs and osprey young end up in the cooking pot. They are on record

as being eaten by Arab Bedouins and in the Cape Verde Islands.

12. Records exist of ospreys drowning, through either refusing to let go of a fish that is stronger than they are or their talons becoming ensnared in a fish as it struggles to escape, dragging them down with it.

13. In West Africa, ospreys lead a more leisurely life than they do when breeding further north. In his PhD dissertation, 'The wintering ecology of the osprey in Senegambia', Y. A. Prevost shows that the birds spend about twelve hours a day roosting or sleeping, an average thirty minutes foraging, another half an hour in flight not connected to hunting and the remainder of the time resting – a deservedly quiet life after their strenuous nesting season.

14. Stamps featuring ospreys appear worldwide. A Belgian Post 2010 special issue depicted six birds of prey – common buzzard, Eurasian hobby, sparrowhawk, red kite, goshawk and osprey – from paintings by wildlife artist André Buzin.

15. The osprey is the official bird of Nova Scotia, where the birds are a common sight. Ospreys return there from their wintering grounds in South America and the Caribbean by mid-April each year. It was depicted on the 1986 series Canadian ten-dollar bill. The osprey is also the official bird of Sudermannia in Sweden.

16. The editor of American *Vogue*, and doyenne of the fashion world, Anna Wintour is not alone in having had an osprey perch built behind her Long Island summerhouse. Once shot and exterminated as vermin, ospreys are now not just geek chic but chic.

17. As solar-powered satellite transmitters add to the general sum of knowledge about wildlife, one young radio-tagged bird from Scotland was recorded as making an incredible non-stop 600-mile journey from Ireland to northern Spain.

18. Ospreys' spring arrival dates at lakes in Sweden, which has about half the European breeding stock, have advanced by some twenty days over the past half a century.

19. According to Roy Dennis, the UK osprey population should be about 2,000 pairs. It is his belief that the osprey will one day once again catch fish on the River Thames in central London.

20. Osprey world population was estimated at 25,000–30,000 breeding pairs by Alan Poole in 1989; nearly two decades later, in 2008, Roy Dennis's estimated 40,000–50,000 pairs shows how the species is flourishing.

Sources and resources

Select bibliography

Brown, Philip, and Waterston, George: *The Return of the Osprey* (Collins, London, 1962)

Burton, Maurice: *Animal Senses* (Routledge & Kegan Paul, London, 1961)

Cocker, Mark, and Mabey, Richard: *Birds Britannia* (Chatto & Windus, London, 2005)

Dennis, Roy: *A Life of Ospreys* (Whittles Publishing, Dunbeath, Scotland, 2008; repr. 2009)

Ferguson-Lees, James, and Christie, David: *Raptors of the World: A field guide*, illus. Franklin, Kim; Mead, David; Burton, Philip; and Harris, Alan (Christopher Helm, London, 2005; repr. 2007)

Gessner, David: *Return of the Osprey: A season of flight and wonder* (Ballantine Books, New York, 2001)

Mynott, Jeremy: *Birdscapes: Birds in our imagination and experience* (Princeton University Press, Princeton and Oxford, 2009)

Poole, Alan F.: *Ospreys: A natural and unnatural history* (Cambridge University Press, Cambridge, 1989)

Prevost, Y. A.: 'The wintering ecology of the ospreys in Senegambia', unpublished PhD dissertation, University of Edinburgh, 1982

Rothschild, Miriam: *Walter Rothschild: The man, the museum and the menagerie* (Natural History Museum, London, 2008)

St John, Charles: *Wild Sports and Natural History of the Highlands* (1845; rev. edn 1892)

Saunders, Howard, and Eagle Clarke, William: *Manual of British Birds* (Gurney and Jackson, Edinburgh, 1927)

Selected websites: UK

British Birds, www.britishbirds.co.uk is a bird journal, published monthly, that features articles on identification, distribution, migration, conservation and taxonomy. It is a place to report significant ornithological sightings and events, and a resource aimed at birders and professional ornithologists. British Birds Rarities Committee (BBRC) publishes its annual report in *British Birds*.

British Ornithologists' Union (BOU), www.bou.org.uk is one of the world's oldest and most respected ornithological organizations, founded in 1858 by scientists including

Professor Alfred Newton FRS. For more than a hundred years BOU has maintained a list of birds recorded in Britain and Ireland. Known as The British List, it featured 592 species in August 2010.

British Trust for Ornithology (BTO), www.bto.org. The BTO has existed since 1933 as an independent, scientific research trust, investigating the populations, movements and ecology of wild birds in the British Isles.

Highland Foundation for Wildlife, www.roydennis.org supports a wide variety of conservation projects and research studies on ospreys.

Rare Breeding Birds Panel (RBBP), www.rbbp.org.uk collects breeding data on the rarer species of birds breeding in the United Kingdom. In 2010, the ospreys featured as a category A on its rare-species list. The RBBP was formed in 1972 by representatives of the RSPB, BTO, The Nature Conservancy Council and *British Birds*.

Royal Society for the Protection of Birds (RSPB), www.rspb.org.uk is Europe's largest wildlife conservation charity. Wildlife and the environment face many threats, and the RSPB's work is focused on the species and habitats that are in the greatest danger. They have more than a million members, over 13,500 volunteers, 1,300 staff and more than 200 nature reserves.

Scottish Wildlife Trust, formed in 1964, is a membership-based registered charity. With more than 36,000 members, 122 wildlife reserves, 21 local groups and a network of dedicated volunteers throughout the country, the Trust aims to 'advance the conservation of Scotland's biodiversity for the benefit of present and future generations'. The charity is affiliated to The Wildlife Trusts, a UK-wide network of 47 Trusts with a combined membership of nearly 800,000.

For more information about the Scottish Wildlife Trust, or to become a member, visit www.swt.org.uk.

Wildlife Extra, www.wildlifeextra.com is an online wildlife magazine for wildlife watchers and lovers and a guide to UK nature reserves.

UK osprey projects

Aberfoyle ospreys, www.forestry.gov.uk/aberfoyleospreys is a Forestry Commission project and part of the Trossachs Bird of Prey Trail.

Kielder Water and Forest Park, www.visitkielder.com stages osprey-watch events and live CCTV coverage from the nest is shown, during the breeding season, at Kielder Castle Visitor Centre. The Kielder Partnership is a public, voluntary and private sector collaboration.

Lake District Osprey Project, www.ospreywatch.co.uk is managed by a partnership of the Forestry Commission, Lake District National Park Authority and the RSPB.

Loch Garten, www.rspb.org.uk/reserves/guide/l/lochgarten /index.aspx at the heart of the beautiful Abernethy Forest, in a location shared with Loch Garten, lies the famous Osprey Centre. Packed with wildlife, bird and tree life, its resident ospreys are to be seen during the months of April to August. For details on satellite tracking of ospreys fledged from the reserve: www.rspb.org.uk/wildlife/tracking/lochgartenospreys/index.aspx

Loch of the Lowes Scottish Wildlife Trust reserve, www.swt.org.uk/visit/visitor-centres/loch-of-the-lowes-visitor-centre. The visitor centre is open all year round. An osprey nest is situated within 150 yards of the observation hides. The ranger service runs a programme of events throughout the season as well as educational activities at Loch of the Lowes.

Rutland Osprey Project, www.ospreys.org.uk is based at Rutland Water. The project is a partnership between the Leicestershire and Rutland Wildlife Trust and Anglian Water, with additional funding support from the Peter De Haan Charitable Trust.

Tweed Valley Osprey Project, www.forestry.gov.uk/tweed valleyospreys, is a partnership involving Forestry Commission Scotland, Kailzie Gardens and the RSPB. The site features an osprey education pack designed for schools.

International websites

Aves de Rapina do Brasil, www.avesderapinabrasil.com features a section on ospreys in South America.

Fascinating osprey migration maps, created by Richard O. Bierregaard, of the Department of Biology at the

University of North Carolina at Charlotte, can be found at www.bioweb.uncc.edu. Bierregaard monitors the migration routes of young ospreys satellite-tagged at nests in Massachusetts and other eastern states of the USA.

BirdLife International, www.birdlife.org is a global partnership of conservation organizations that strives to conserve birds, their habitats and global biodiversity, working with people towards sustainability in the use of natural resources.

Cornell Laboratory of Ornithology, www.birds.cornell.edu is involved with exploring and conserving the natural world. Its mission is to interpret and conserve the Earth's biological diversity through research, education and citizen science focused on birds. Webcam images and information about ospreys: www.birds.cornell.edu/bird house/nestboxcam

www.europeanraptors.org/raptors/osprey.html includes the biology and conservation of all diurnal raptor species regularly found in Europe.

Global Raptor Information Network (GRIN), www.global raptors.org is designed to provide information on diurnal raptors (hawks, eagles and falcons) and to facilitate communication between raptor researchers and organizations interested in the conservation of these species.

International Osprey Foundation, www.ospreys.com is US-based and has an excellent photo gallery. Its focus is on education and conservation.

League for the Protection of Birds (LPO) Mission Rapaces, Balbuzard Pecheur, balbuzard.lpo.fr is a group dedicated to raptor conservation in France.

OspreyWorld, www.ospreyworld.com launched by David Gessner, is intended as both an introduction for beginners and a place for osprey followers to learn more and exchange ideas. It features a guest column by Alan F. Poole.

Visual Resources for Ornithology or VIREO, www.vireo. acnatsci.org is the worldwide bird photograph collection of the US Academy of the Natural Sciences. It features more than 150,000 photographs representing at least 7,000 species and has a comprehensive collection of ornithological images, including osprey photos.

To hear osprey, try www.xeno-canto.org for bird songs from around the world. The RSPB website, www.rspb. org.uk also features vocalizations for all bird species featured there.

International osprey webcams

There are many of them. Here are a few to try:

Connecticut Audubon Society: www.ctaudubon.org/action/osprey.htm

Dunedin osprey cam, Florida: www.dunedinospreycam.com

Finnish Museum of Natural History, University of Finland, has a website www.luomus.fi/english/zoology/satelliteospreys/jukka devoted to satellite-tracking ospreys.

www.friendsofblackwater.org/friends.html The Friends of Blackwater is a non-profit citizens' support group, assisting Blackwater National Wildlife Refuge in Cambridge, Maryland, and the Chesapeake Marshlands National Wildlife Refuge Complex. For ospreys nesting on Blackwater reserve: www.friendsofblackwater.org/camcentral.html

Acknowledgements

To Chelsey Fox, my agent, who first drew my attention to Lady, for her wisdom, wit and help throughout. To Valerie Coughlin, who introduced us, and Patrick Coughlin for Chealsea Arts Club Ramblers. To Andreas Campomar, editorial director, Constable & Robinson, and Martin Palmer, group sales and marketing director, for their belief. To Leo Hollis, for his keen, expert editorial and authorial eye. To Hazel Orme, a skilled editor with whom I have worked before and have been fortunate to do so again. To Jo Stansall, Emily Burns and the team at Constable, for their patience and support. To Gary Nutting, for reading and re-reading of early drafts, for his journalistic eye and insight, and George Chamier, knowledgeable about raptors, birds and Scotland, who kindly read an early version of the book. To Peter Ferns and the Scottish Wildlife Trust for their cooperation, expert reading of the typescript and, most crucially, their vital conservation work with ospreys that has helped Lady and the osprey to thrive.